'Dr. Owojaiye is fast becoming one of the most outstanding evangelical voices on the African continent. He gracefully combines his skills as an exceptional Christian thinker and as a sound pastoral practitioner. This book is a product of his rich reflections on the impact of the coronavirus restrictions on corporate worship in Nigeria. The book offers fresh insights into the future of evangelical Christianity in Africa. I enthusiastically commend it to you.'
– *Georges P. Atido, Professor of World Christianity and Missiology and President, Shalom University, Bunia, Democratic Republic of Congo.*

'Dr. Owojaiye's book provides, not only a timely response to the current pandemic, but also a much wider lens with which to view the disease. He approaches the subject from the rich perspective of World Christianity as viewed by someone positioned in the majority world. I commend his unique effort to the reader.'
– *Mark R. Shaw, Professor of Historical Studies and Director, Center for World Christianity, Africa International University, Nairobi, Kenya.*

'The author has used the example of ECWA as a hook around which to have a wide-ranging discussion of issues facing Christians in Africa today. I commend it to you.'
– *Paul Todd, Publishing Editor, Africa Christian Textbooks (ACTS) and Deputy Director, SIM Nigeria.*

'This book on the unfolding apocalyptic phenomenon of COVID-19 is an important initiative. Babatomiwa Owojaiye breaks ground for what promises to be a thriving motif for intellectual endeavours for generations to come. The book is engaging, lucid reading and reminds the church about its unique role in history, especially in the face of plagues and pandemics (suffering)—when the core tenets of love, care, sacrifice with courage and hope—shine out the brightest. I heartily commend it for the consideration of the church in Africa and beyond.'
– *Aiah Foday-Khabenje, General Secretary, Association for Evangelicals in Africa, Nairobi, Kenya.*

'This is a groundbreaking eyewitness study on the COVID-19 pandemic from the majority world. Its beauty lies in its multidisciplinary approach to the subject matter. The book is an indispensable primer for all who seek to understand the impact of the coronavirus lockdowns on how church is done in Africa. It is a must-read for scholars, leaders and all who seek wisdom to fulfil the mission of God in this new normal era of the world.'
– **Stephen O.Y. Baba, ECWA Clergy, Professor of Biblical Studies and former Provost, ECWA Theological Seminary, Igbaja, Nigeria.**

EVANGELICAL RESPONSE TO THE CORONAVIRUS LOCKDOWN

(Insights from the Evangelical Church Winning All)

Babatomiwa M. Owojaiye

WestBow Press
A DIVISION OF THOMAS NELSON
& ZONDERVAN

Copyright © 2020 Babatomiwa M. Owojaiye.

All rights reserved. No part of this book may be used or reproduced by any means, graphic, electronic, or mechanical, including photocopying, recording, taping or by any information storage retrieval system without the written permission of the author except in the case of brief quotations embodied in critical articles and reviews.

WestBow Press books may be ordered through booksellers or by contacting:

WestBow Press
A Division of Thomas Nelson & Zondervan
1663 Liberty Drive
Bloomington, IN 47403
www.westbowpress.com
1 (866) 928-1240

Because of the dynamic nature of the Internet, any web addresses or links contained in this book may have changed since publication and may no longer be valid. The views expressed in this work are solely those of the author and do not necessarily reflect the views of the publisher, and the publisher hereby disclaims any responsibility for them.

Any people depicted in stock imagery provided by Getty Images are models, and such images are being used for illustrative purposes only.
Certain stock imagery © Getty Images.

Scripture quotations marked (NIV) are taken from the Holy Bible, New International Version®, NIV®. Copyright © 1973, 1978, 1984, 2011 by Biblica, Inc.® Used by permission of Zondervan. All rights reserved worldwide. www.zondervan.com The "NIV" and "New International Version" are trademarks registered in the United States Patent and Trademark Office by Biblica, Inc.®

Scripture marked (ICB) taken from the International Children's Bible®. Copyright © 1986, 1988, 1999 by Thomas Nelson. Used by permission. All rights reserved.

Scripture quotations marked (NLT) are taken from the Holy Bible, New Living Translation, copyright ©1996, 2004, 2015 by Tyndale House Foundation. Used by permission of Tyndale House Publishers, a Division of Tyndale House Ministries, Carol Stream, Illinois 60188. All rights reserved.

ISBN: 978-1-9736-9755-8 (sc)
ISBN: 978-1-9736-9757-2 (hc)
ISBN: 978-1-9736-9756-5 (e)

Library of Congress Control Number: 2020913051

Print information available on the last page.

WestBow Press rev. date: 7/29/2020

CONTENTS

Dedication vii
Abbreviations ix
Acknowledgement xi
Foreword xv

CHAPTER 1: Setting the Stage 1
CHAPTER 2: Conspiracy Theories, Covid-19 Lockdown and
              Average Nigerians 18
CHAPTER 3: Evangelical Christianity in Africa 35
CHAPTER 4: Pentecostal and Evangelical Christianity in
              Africa: Soulmates or Strange Bedfellows? 53
CHAPTER 5: Essential Elements of Corporate
              Worship in ECWA 75
CHAPTER 6: Coronavirus Lockdown and Corporate
              Worship in ECWA 100
CHAPTER 7: Evangelical Response to Coronavirus
              Lockdown: the Case of ECWA 111
CHAPTER 8: Insights for the Future of ECWA 127
CHAPTER 9: Implications for the Church in Africa 147

Bibliography 165
Scripture Reference 187
General Index 191

DEDICATION

To Boaz, my uncle, who believed in me and was used by God to help me chart a path in ministry.

To my children, Bísádé, Bùsólámi, and Bámisè for your support, endurance, friendship and godliness.

To Bíódún, for your godly character, love, support, prayers, and for being an awesome sweetheart. "Many women do noble things, but you surpass them all" (Proverbs 31:29, NIV). You are special!

And to all of God's children everywhere.

ABBREVIATIONS

AIC	-	Africa Inland Church
A&E	-	Accident and Emergency Unit
AoG	-	The Assemblies of God
AMORC	-	Ancient and Mystical Order Rosae Crucis
BBC	-	British Broadcasting Corporation
AMS	-	African Missionary Society
AEA	-	Association for Evangelicals in Africa
DLBC	-	Deeper Life Bible Church
CAN	-	Christian Association of Nigeria
CBCAfrica	-	Centre for Biblical Christianity in Africa
CITAM	-	Christ is the Answer Ministries
COCIN	-	Church of Christ in Nations
COVID-19	-	Coronavirus disease 2019
DCC	-	District Church Council
ECWA	-	Evangelical Church Winning All

ELWA	-	Eternal Love Winning All
EPL	-	ECWA Productions Limited
ELWWA	-	Eternal Love Will Win All
EMS	-	Evangelical Missionary Society
FCT	-	Federal Capital Territory
FESTIGOS	-	Festival of Gospel Songs
FGCN	-	Foursquare Gospel Church in Nigeria
GCC	-	General Church Council
ICT	-	Information Communication Technology
LC	-	Local Church
LCC	-	Local Church Council
NAE	-	National Association of Evangelicals
NBC	-	National Broadcasting Commission
NBC	-	National Bureau of Statistics
NBC	-	Nigerian Baptist Convention
NCC	-	Nigerian Communications Commission
NCDC	-	National Centre for Disease Control
NMA	-	Nigeria Medical Association
PHEIC	-	Public Health Emergency of International Concern
UITH	-	University of Ilorin Teaching Hospital
WASSC	-	West African Senior School Certificate
WEA	-	World Evangelical Alliance
WHO	-	World Health Organization
RCCG	-	Redeemed Christian Church of God
SIM	-	Sudan Interior Mission (now Serving in Mission)
SU	-	Scripture Union
UMCA	-	United Missionary Church of Africa

ACKNOWLEDGEMENT

I have met three kinds of people in life and in my Christian pilgrimage–those who have discouraged me; those who are indifferent about me or whatever life throws at me; and those who have challenged, encouraged and helped '*fan into flames the gifts of God in me*' (2 Timothy 1: 6, NIV). In any case, they all have continued to serve to the accomplishment of the purpose of God in and for my life. This book would not have been possible without the support of people who have challenged, nudged and encouraged me to undertake this project. These *encouragers* are too many to list here, but let me highlight just a few. Some proceeds from my unpublished theses and works form a small part of this book. So, for this, my appreciation goes to my supervisors: Professors Abiodun Ige, Zacchaeus Apata, Mark Shaw, Diane Stinton, Mark Fackler, Gyang Pam and James Obrempong-Nkansah for their tutelage and contributions at every stage of my student life and theses writing. My special thanks goes to Professor Mark Shaw. My interest in World Christianity was borne out of my contact with this erudite scholar and mentor in September 2009 at Africa International University in Nairobi, Kenya. And ever since, my love for the discipline has continued to wax stronger.

I take this opportunity to also register my unreserved gratitude to Professor Julius Owoyemi, Dr. Wanjiru M. Gitau, Engineer Seun Bolaji, Dr. Olaleke Folaranmi, Mrs. Bola Oludele and Mrs. Wanjiku Joyce Mwangi for reading through this work and for their immense contributions towards its success. Joyce Mwangi's support in this project was phenomenal, to say the least. Thank you for your friendship, Joyce. I acknowledge the encouragements of Pastor Eli and Mabel Alasan, Pastor Samuel and Mrs. Mary Jolayemi and Reverend Stephen and Mrs. Oluwakemi Ajise (my *bosses* at First ECWA, Ilorin) at every stage of this writing. My special thanks goes to the membership and leadership of First ECWA, Ilorin, Ilorin District Church Council and ECWA as a whole for giving me the environment, platform and latitude to grow in the grace of God. I thank all the members of the Centre for Biblical Christianity in Africa (CBCAfrica) team for labouring with us in our mission to deepen the roots of biblical Christianity and widen the transformative impact of the Christian message in the African public square. Thank you and may the Lord bless you all exceedingly.

To my children, Bisade, Bùsólámi and Bámisè: thank you so much for your understanding and support every step of the way. I salute my wife, Biodun. I owe you so much. I appreciate your deep love, unflinching support, and understanding for me always. *Eku management wa o!* Thank you especially for allowing me to use the time I should have spent with you and the children on this project. Your understanding and support cheered me to this point.

What would I ever do without your support? May God reward you abundantly. My final appreciation goes to God, the giver of life and every good gift. I thank him for his unimaginable and unceasing love towards me and for granting me the grace to undertake this project. Without him I am nothing! *Olúwa, modúpé o!*

FOREWORD

The coronavirus disease has unexpectedly blindsided the whole world within a very short period of time. It has been shocking to see self-assured, developed western nations, even worst hit than Africa, reeling in social, economic and religious confusion in the aftermath of this globally indiscriminate disease. It is therefore very encouraging to see the remarkable work rising to the occasion out of Africa to help people come to terms with the disruption brought to humanity by this disease. This book is a high-quality, timely response prepared from the perspective of one Evangelical tradition, ECWA, set within the broader context of Nigeria and the mission of the church in Africa, generally. Indeed, Babatomiwa's approach shows that the coronavirus has, not so much introduced new problems; rather, the disease has opened up wounds and scars we never bothered to heal properly.

The book goes into remarkable depth to highlight such things as the church's response to disease throughout history. Did you know that whenever epidemics occurred, Christians would be at the forefront of infection and contagion caring for the sick, even to the cost of their own lives? Babatomiwa opines that the church has always been part of the solution by offering unconditional love, sacrificial care, hope and brave witness. Even now in the year of our Lord 2020, the call of the deep unto deep is no different, and the fastest growing church in the world, the African church, cannot fail the test at this moment. Moses leads us to realize that the church has its God-given responsibility to maintain the spiritual nurture of its members and at the same time, extend itself to meet new challenges that it was not prepared for. As the missiologist David Bosch observes in his book, *Transforming Mission: Paradigm Shifts in Theology of Mission (1991)* by using Hendrik Kraemer's words, '... the church is always in a ... crisis, and ... its greatest shortcoming is that it is only occasionally aware of it.' Bosch continues quoting Kramer adding, the church 'has always needed ... suffering in order to become fully alive to its real nature and mission.' Well, the suffering is here, and Brother Moses invites us, the church, to be aware of both contingency and crisis and to respond as a community committed to partnering with its Lord, to heal the broken-hearted, to bind up the wounded and continue to bring good news of the kingdom.

    This is not just a book about the coronavirus. The work takes unexpected angles that reveal both the pastoral heart and scholarly mind of the author. He does a rounded exposition of evangelicalism and its relationship to Pentecostalism, particularly in its Nigerian expressions. There are dimensions of the contemporary circumstances of the church in Africa, both within the ecclesial circles and in the public sphere, that have been addressed by other scholars in whose footsteps Moses walks. The work has the potential to refresh conversations on stale debates in scholarship, matters such as prosperity theology, unhealthy denominationalism and ecumenism. I particularly like how Moses starts to point us towards revisiting the idea of Pan-Africanism, particularly as it might be expressed in the east African ideal of ubuntu, which itself invites us all to sit in and have a village palaver to eat together and listen to each other. Perchance, we might rediscover that in unity, we will be able to surmount the jaded image and content with which our mother continent is held abroad.

I invite you to join Brother Babatomiwa Moses Owojaiye as he sees this deadly challenge of COVID-19 as an opportunity to introspect on long-term, deep-seated issues that the church in Africa needs to face up to. Together, we can address them so we can pursue long-term missional impact, even in our continuously changing and dizzying world. May the Lord bless these "five loaves of bread and two fish" (Matthew 14:17, NIV) into a meal to feed thousands with knowledge and wisdom on how to act in these disruptive times.

Wanjiru M. Gitau, Ph.D.
Senior Research Scholar, St. Thomas University, Miami, Florida
Author, *Megachurch Christianity Reconsidered:
Millennials and Social Change in African Perspective*

CHAPTER ONE
SETTING THE STAGE

How the journey started. It was a sunny Sunday afternoon on November 4. I had just returned from church and was bored in the room I had rented in Isanlu-Isin, a town in Kwara State of Nigeria. I had traveled to Isanlu-Isin as a private student to take the West African Senior School Certificate (WASSC) examination. Previously, I had attempted the examination and failed when I was a student living in central Nigeria. As a result, I went to a place where I was not known to retest. I needed a different atmosphere to avoid being seen as a failure by residents, friends and colleagues in the community where I had initially completed the examination.

I lived alone in this new community. Although I came to this new town in order to fully concentrate on my studies, there were times I felt quite lonely and needed some fresh air. I attended church on Sundays to reduce the boredom, and change my environment. Although I grew up in a Christian family, I did not know what it meant to have a personal salvation experience with Jesus - I was a reckless young man. Whereas many members of my immediate and extended family were not Christians, they were worried about the way-ward life I was living. I was equally aware of my reckless ways but was not yet ready to toe the line of the so-called "born-again" Christians. On that fateful Sunday, after I had returned from church and taken lunch, I grew tired of reading and needed a distraction. The thought of going to watch a television program came to me. I went to the home of one of my neighbors, one of the very few families that had the privilege of owning a black-and-white television set in the neighborhood. The home was always bubbling with throngs of people coming to watch soaps or other programmes being aired on the television.

As I watched the television, a Christian film produced by a new Christian film industry, the Evangelical Vineyard Outreach Ministry (EVOM) World Outreach was being aired. Usually in Nigeria, a government-owned television like the one I was watching would broadcast Islamic or Christian content for a lengthy period only on Fridays and Sundays, unless it was the festive season. It was not uncommon, however, for a Christian film to air for ninety minutes on a Sunday.

The movie I watched was a newly released Christian film entitled, *Olugbala Gba Mi* (Rescue, Deliver or Save me, Lord). The film was written and produced in the Yoruba language. It took place in a typical urban settlement of Southwest Nigeria, and the story was about Banji and Boye, two city boys caught in a web of sin and worldliness. They were involved in uncivil activities. The boys grew in their sinfulness and reckless lifestyles until they encountered an elderly man, Pa Josiah, who spoke to them about Jesus Christ and the need to commit their lives to him. Banji and Boye's encounter with Pa Josiah led them to a conversion experience which brought significant transformation into their lives.

Their story struck me like a thunderbolt. As I watched the movie, it appeared as though it were story. I identified with the boys. Watching *Olugbala Gba Mi* birthed a major turning point in my life. This story marks the beginning of my journey in evangelical Christianity. I am still on the journey about three decades later. This book is more than just an academic interest for me. I am an evangelical Christian affiliated to the Evangelical Church Winning All (ECWA). I write as an insider who seeks to understand and inform others about the effects of Coronavirus disease 2019 (COVID-19) lockdown on corporate worship in ECWA and to offer helpful insights on the practice of Evangelical Christianity in ECWA and the wider African church going forward in the light of this new global reality. However, as you will later discover, I did not allow my affiliation to ECWA becloud the scholarly objectivity and rigour required for this kind of work.

Welcoming an Unwanted Visitor

Since the first outbreak of COVID-19 in China, the people of the Ilorin metropolis, where I reside with my family did not feel the scary, ravaging and deadly impact of the pandemic until two index cases in our city were confirmed by the National Centre for Disease Control (NCDC) and announced through a press statement on Monday April 6, 2020 by Rafiu Ajakaye, the Chief Press Secretary to the Executive Governor of Kwara State and the Spokesman of the Technical Committee on COVID-19. The tension became more aggravated when the Executive Governor of Kwara State,

Abdulrahman Abdulrazaq, made a press briefing the following day. While the press briefing instilled hope, courage and faith in the populace, the confirmation of the arrival of the pandemic in Kwara State by the governor came with a thick sense of fear and confusion among the residents of the state. The index cases in Kwara State came about two months after Nigeria's index case was reported in Lagos on the February 27, 2020. Shortly after the national index case in Lagos, additional cases were gradually detected and confirmed in Ogun, Ekiti, Oyo, Edo, Bauchi, Osun, the Federal Capital Territory (FCT) Abuja, Enugu, Kaduna, Benue, Akwa Ibom, and Ondo State, respectively. These states had confirmed cases of COVID-19 before that of Kwara, and before long, the presence of coronavirus was felt in almost every state in Nigeria.

Despite the accelerating spread of COVID-19 in Nigeria and globally, there was still a great sense of denial and security amongst the residents of Kwara State until the dreadful news of its arrival was confirmed on April 6, 2020. Since then, Kwara State has changed and might never be the same again. Of course, before this day, there was already a great sense of uneasiness following the ban of free human movement and large gatherings of people in the state precipitated by the national index case in Lagos. Partial lockdown and social distancing were part of the measures prescribed by the federal and state governments to prevent and contain the spread of coronavirus. Residents of the state endured the attending burdens of COVID-19 until the state's index cases were reported. The majority of the populace considered the process that led to the arrival of the pandemic in the state careless and irresponsible.

The alleged smuggling and management of a fifty-seven year old United Kingdom returnee, Muideen Obanimomo, into the University of Ilorin Teaching Hospital (UITH) by a professor of medicine, Professor Salami Alakija Kazeem of the same hospital, stirred an outrage amongst the residents of Ilorin, in particular, and the state, in general. The outburst was allegedly caused by the perceived unethical and unprofessional manner with which Professor Salami handled an alleged COVID-19 patient in the state. The density of the outrage could be felt on the social media and in the press briefing made by the state governor. This development eventually led to the immediate suspension of Professor Salami Alakija Kazeem by the authorities of the University of Ilorin Teaching Hospital.

Investigative Journalist Fisayo Soyombo had alleged through a media report that the Kwara State Government, authorities of UITH and Professor Salami Alakija Kazeem were in a conspiracy against the people of the state in an attempt to cover-up Muideen Obanimomo's COVID-19 case.[1] According to his report, Muideen Obanimomo flew into Nigeria from the United Kingdom through the Muritala International Airport in Lagos on March 20, 2020. Suspecting that he might have contracted the virus, he went into brief isolation in Lagos. Muideen Obanimomo's condition deteriorated days into his isolation in Lagos. Following this unfortunate development, Professor Salami, a cousin to Muideen Obanimono, was contacted, and he advised that Muideen be brought to Ilorin for further investigation and close monitoring. Muideen Obanimomo set foot in Ilorin in the company of his wife on Sunday March 29, 2020. At that point, his condition had further worsened. Now under the alleged management of Professor Salami, Muideen Obanimomo was taken to one or two hospitals in Ilorin before he finally ended up in UITH Accident and Emergency Unit (A&E). On getting there, Professor Salami Kazeem as senior staff

---

[1] Fasayo Soyombo, 'The Grand Coronavirus Cover-Up in Kwara' in https://www.thecable.ng/the-grand-coronavirus-cover-up-in-kwara, Posted on April 6, 2020, Accessed on April 8, 2020. Soyombo was former Editor of *TheCable; the International Centre for Investigative Reporting (ICIR);* and *SaharaReporters.*

and specialist muzzled his social capital to secure other health workers on duty to provide immediate attention to his client. It was reported that after some observations, the health workers on duty suspected that the symptoms presented by the patient were similar to that of COVID-19. But Professor Salami was quick to dispel their suspicion, claiming that the case was food poisoning and not COVID-19. Muideen Obanimomo died a few hours after his arrival and treatment at UITH. Allegedly, Professor Salami went on to process the immediate release of the corpse for burial in accordance to Islamic rites. The corpse was released and the burial was conducted almost immediately.[2]

The outrage was heightened by people's knowledge about the calibre of the physician that Salami Alakija Kazeem was. Fisayo Soyombo lamented that 'Professor Abdulsalam is not just a physician. He is an academic in the fields of respiratory medicine with research interest in infectious and non-infectious pulmonary diseases such as tuberculosis, obstructive airways diseases and HIV/AIDS. A physician and an academic of this calibre would have gotten Obanimomo tested if he genuinely wanted to. The failure to test Obanimomo for COVID-19 until his death and afterwards has cover-up written all over it.'[3] Professor Salami was allegedly expected to have known and managed the case better. People became more suspicious when the wife of Muideen Obanimomo later tested positive for COVID-19. It was at this point that the seriousness of the allegations, as well as the magnitude of the unfortunate development, dawned on the leadership and residents of the state. Could Mrs Obanimomo's case be a coincidence or an isolated development? Meanwhile, the Kwara State Government

---

[2] Ibid.

[3] Fasayo Soyombo, 'The Grand Coronavirus Cover-Up in Kwara'

and the authorities of UITH had denied any involvement in the matter, but that did not stop the dreaded hand of coronavirus from reaching Kwara State.

It should be on record that as much as a majority of the Kwara State residents believed that Professor Salami Alakija Kazeem was culpable, there was no hard evidence to ascertain that Muideen Obanimomo died of COVID-19. Later, Mrs Obanimono also tested negative after being isolated and treated by the state government. This narrative serves to picture the distinctiveness of my context and people's initial responses to the arrival of the coronavirus pandemic. However, it is essential to clarify that this reaction was peculiar to Kwara State and may not be generalisable for the whole of Nigeria. Certainly, reactions are different from one context to another.

Nothing has challenged human existence in the twenty-first century more than the scourge of coronavirus, otherwise known as COVID-19. The coronavirus pandemic has brought upon the world a global health crisis of unprecedented proportion. It has touched on every aspect of human life and society. It has shaken the world in a nuanced, complex and complicated dimension. It is definitely not an overstatement to say that its impact has been felt in ways beyond human description. COVID-19 has, in one way or the other, affected every human being, community, society and nation in our modern world. Therefore, for obvious reasons, no single study can adequately describe the various ways that the pandemic has affected our contemporary world. It would be a daunting task to attempt to provide a detailed narrative of the unprecedented impact of COVID-19 on mankind in a single study.

Being a new and an evolving discourse in the fields of human inquiry, the subject could be studied from a multi-dimensional perspective. It could be studied from an educational, religious, theological, sociological, missiological, medical, scientific, technological, biological, financial, economic, leadership and governance perspectives, to highlight just a few. Going forward, scholarly writings on this subject will begin to appear. This is a new journey in scholarship that will continue over a long period of time. Therefore, writing on Coronavirus will depend on the perspective that the researcher is focusing on. One common and fundamental denominator in the discourse of the impact of COVID-19 is that it has left an indelible mark on the world and in the sands of history. The world is never going to be the same again following the outbreak of the pandemic.

Just as it is the case with every facet of human life and existence, COVID-19 has also posed unprecedented challenges to the nature and operations of religion globally. Coronavirus has now become one of the greatest *enemies* of religion. While religion promotes the gathering and social interaction of human being, COVID-19 promotes the dispelling of the same. Coronavirus is a scourge that killed several thousands of people within a relatively short period of time. The pandemic succeeded in challenging human greatness. Human ingenuity, education, wealth, science, research and technology put together are too frail to immediately help confront the scourge of COVID-19. Needless to say that advanced, wealthy, technologically savvy, militarily advanced and organized societies around the world were brought down on their knees by this pandemic. In order to reduce its impact on human existence, the measures of banning free human movement and convergence in large number had to be sustained through lockdowns. This singular development has affected the way religion is being practiced generally and evangelical spirituality specifically.

Religious leaders and adherents have devised means to keep their faiths afloat. While some changes have been mild, others have been complex and revolutionary. The impact has been further complicated by the sudden shift from traditional ways of practicing religion and the prolonged nature of the same. As sudden as the introduction of these new changes in religious practices may appear, most of these changes have come to stay. Invariably, we must begin to adjust ourselves to the new ways of practicing our faiths in the contexts of our new local and global realities.

This book is one of the earliest of such to come out from Africa. It is a case study research that focused primarily on the Evangelical Church Winning All (ECWA). Whereas the membership of ECWA spreads beyond the shore of Nigeria, the scope of this study is confined to ECWA in Nigeria only. This book examines the effects of the Coronavirus lockdown on corporate worship in ECWA and discusses the response of the denomination to the same. Even though the scope of the study is zoomed on ECWA, the implications of our findings in our investigation of the denomination is generalisable and extrapolated to the wider church in Africa. These implications are important for the future of Evangelical Christianity in Africa. I have employed the term Evangelical in an open, inclusive and generous sense to accommodate the Pentecostal/Charismatic movement in Africa. Significant attention is given in the book to describe the relationship between Evangelical and Pentecostal/Charismatic movements, as well as their place within the African Christian tapestry. I am aware that the outbreak of COVID-19 pandemic came with a wide spectrum of opportunities and challenges. But this book focuses more on the adverse effects of Coronavirus lockdown rather than the opportunities it has created. The ban on religious gathering in Nigeria started in March and ended in June 2020. It lasted for a minimum period of sixteen weeks, depending on the peculiarities of each federating unit of Nigeria.

COVID-19: A Strange Disease Ravaging Nations

COVID-19 is an acronym derived from the words 'coronavirus disease 2019'. The disease was labeled as a public health emergency of international concern (PHEIC) on January 30, 2020, but the official name for the virus was announced on February 11, 2020 by the World Health Organization (WHO) as Severe Acute Respiratory Syndrome Corona Virus (SARS-CoV-2 2019).[4] It has infected millions of people and has been responsible for the death of hundreds of thousands of people around the world.

In December 2019, just a month before the Chinese spring festival, an outbreak of a strange disease was reported at the Huanan Seafood wet market located in Wuhan, Hubei, China. This disease presented mainly with respiratory symptoms which spread and affected about two-thirds of the workers. The early cases of COVID-19 all had exposure to the seafood market; this is regarded as the primary spread. The majority of the spread was by secondary spread i.e. human to human transmission as evidenced by illness in those without contact with the Wuhan market or wild life and by the transmission of the infection from patients to healthcare workers. Within a month of the report of this disease in Wuhan, it spread to the rest of the country and beyond, involving countries like Thailand, Japan, Republic of Korea, Singapore, Germany and the United States. By the end of March, 2020, the disease had been recorded in 177 countries. And by April, 2020, the United States of America became the hardest hit country and the global epicenter of the pandemic in terms of the number of casualties who tested positive to the virus and those who died by the same.

---

[4] Tim Jewell, 'Everything you should know about the 2019 Coronavirus and COVID-19' in *Healthline*: https://www.healthline.com/health/coronavirus-covid-19/ Posted on April 23, 2020; Accessed on April 25, 2020.

The most commonly reported symptoms are persistent fever, body aches, fatigue and cough, with frequent involvement of the lower respiratory tracts. Less common symptoms include headache and diarrhoea. Currently, there is no standard treatment, and vaccine development is still underway. The most effective way to control this outbreak is to prevent infection and curtail spread through personal hygiene, regular washing of hands with soap or alcohol-based hand sanitizer, social distancing and bans on large human gatherings and free movement. The outbreak in China occurred just prior to its largest annual cultural event; the Lunar New Year, a holiday that is usually characterized by a massive migration of people traveling in crowded vehicles for long periods of time. The Chinese government had little time to act before a large-scale disaster would evolve. They deployed traditional public health response tactics which included isolation of infected people, quarantine of exposed persons and enforcement of social distancing. This led to a total lockdown of free human movements, gathering and public facilities. The Chinese approach become a template for the prevention and containment of the disease globally. But, in less than six months, the disease has been responsible for the deaths of several people and drove the economies and health care systems of many nations in the world aground. There are ongoing theories challenging the authenticity of the Chinese government's claim that COVID-19 originated from a seafood market in Wuhan, China. Obviously, there is a lot to be heard about this deadly disease in future.

Most countries in the African continent, especially West Africa, have poorly funded healthcare structure and will be unable to upscale to meet the needs required to combat an epidemic. In this region, the health expenditure per capita is lower than $80, with fewer than five hospital beds available per ten thousand of the population. The crippling impact of this pandemic has been seen in countries with advanced healthcare institutions, especially the United States, Italy and Spain with health expenditure per capita of $10,246, $2,840 and $2,506 respectively.[5] By extrapolation, and according to many projections, the impact of this pandemic on Africa could be devastating if strict control measures aimed at minimising the spread of COVID-19 are not enforced.

Church's Responses to Plagues in History

No doubt, COVID-19 is a plague of monumental proportions, and it will continue to occupy a towering space in the history of global health crises. This is due to the amount of pain and opportunities it has visited upon the modern world. But the coronavirus outbreak is not the first pandemic to ravage the world. Historians have documented at least four great plagues that devastated the world before the coronavirus pandemic. What were the responses of the church to the pandemics? Let us now briefly consider those that happened during the second, third, fourteenth and nineteenth centuries of the Christian era.

The Antonine Plague

The Antonine plague is otherwise known in history as the Plague of Galen. This plague, according to historian John Horgan, 'erupted in 165 CE at the height of Roman power throughout the Mediterranean world during the reign of . . . Emperor Marcus Aurelius Antoninus

---

[5] 'Current Health Expenditure per Capita (Current US$) | Data.' Word Health Organisation Global Health Expenditure Database in *The World Bank*: 2015. https://data.worldbank.org/indicator/SH.XPD.CHEX.PC.CD/ Accessed April 25, 2020.

(161-180 CE).⁶ The outbreak came in two phases. The first phase lasted for fifteen years from 165 to 180 CE; while the second outbreak occurred from 251 to 266 CE. A Greek physician who was an eye-witness to the outbreak described the common symptoms of the plague as 'fever, diarrhea, vomiting, thirstiness, swollen throat, and coughing . . . the diarrhea appeared blackish which suggested gastrointestinal bleeding. The coughing produced a foul odour on the breath and exanthema, skin eruptions or rash, over the entirety of the body distinguished by red and black papules or eruptions.'⁷ The disease lasted for two weeks before killing its victim. Although not all its victims died, the Antonine Plague was responsible for the death of about two thousand to five thousand - persons per day (at the peak of the outbreak), and about 10% of the 75 million people in the Roman Empire in total.⁸ Scholars argued that the disease emerged from what is known today as China when the Roman military came into contact with the disease during the siege of Seleucia.⁹ Studies have suggested that the plague could be smallpox. Historians observed that the outbreak of the Antonine Plague was the beginning of the fall of the Roman Empire.

Christian response to the plague was that of love, care and sacrifice. Instead of worshipping the *Alexikakos*, the Averter of Evil erected by the authorities of the Roman Empire, Christians in Anatolian town of Hierapolis risked being persecuted by directing

---

⁶ John Horgan, 'Antonine Plague' in *Ancient History Encyclopedia*: https://www.ancient.eu/Antonine_Plague/ Posted on May 2, 2019.

⁷ Ibid.

⁸ Lyman Stone, 'Christianity Has Been Handling Epidemics for 2000 Years' in *Foreign Policy*: https://foreignpolicy.com/2020/03/13/christianity-epidemics-2000-years-should-i-still-go-to-church-coronavirus/ Posted on March 13, 2020, Accessed on May 5, 2020.

⁹ John Horgan, 'Antonine Plague.'

their neighbours to the true source of life, Jesus.[10] They did this through their display of unconditional love and sacrificial care. According to Lyman Stone, '. . . as Christians cared for the sick and offered a spiritual model whereby plagues were not the work of angry and capricious deities but the product of a broken creation in revolt against a loving God,'[11] their actions challenged age-long worldviews, because people were able to view life and death in a completely new way. Quoting Rodney Stark, Lyman Stone explains that "the death rates in the cities with Christian communities may have been just half that of other cities."[12] Their biblical actions of love and evangelism paid off in that they served to convert many to Christianity. This gave Christianity credibility and led to the spread of the emerging faith in the Roman Empire. Hitherto, the Christian faith and its adherents had suffered terrible persecutions in the Roman world.

The Plague of Cyprian

According to Historian John Horgan, The Plague of Cyprian erupted near Ethiopia in 250 CE and reached Rome, Greece and Syria the following year. The spread of the plague was helped by the incessant wars commonly fought around that time. The armed forces of the various nations in the region facilitated the spread unintentionally. The Plague of Cyprian lasted twenty years and was reported to have

---

[10] Edwards Watts, 'What Rome Learned from the Deadly Antonine Plague of 165 A.D' in *Smithsonian Magazine*: https://www.smithsonianmag.com/history/what-rome-learned-deadly-antonine-plague-165-d-180974758/ Published on April 28, 2020, Accessed on May 5, 2020.

[11] Lyman Stone, 'Christianity Has Been Handling Epidemics for 2000 Years.'

[12] Ibid. See also Rodney Stark, *The Rise of Christianity: a Sociologist Reconsiders History* (New Jersey: Princeton University Press, 1996).

killed at its peak as many as five thousand 5000 people per day in Rome.¹³ Horgan explained that the 'sufferers experienced bouts of diarrhoea, continuous vomiting, fever, deafness, blindness, paralysis of their legs and feet, swollen throats and blood filled their eyes (conjunctival bleeding) while staining their mouths. More often than not, death resulted.'¹⁴ By this time, the Christian responses and worldviews introduced during the Antonine Plague had gained significant prominence. And so, it was much easier for the church to respond just as they did during the initial plague.

The Bubonic plague

The Bubonic plague otherwise known as Black Death broke out in Europe killing over 50 million people. According to the World Health Organisation, the disease 'is transmitted . . . by the bite of infected fleas.'¹⁵ The infective organism is called Yersinia pestis. Scott W. Sunquist records that "the plague was brought to Europe in 1330 from China via rats and fleas."¹⁶ When the Bubonic plague hit Wittenberg in 1527, Christians in the city also confronted the disease with unmatched dedication to duty and sacrificial care for the victims, irrespective of religious affiliations. While non-Christians were fleeing from the pandemic, Christians in Wittenberg were

---

[13] John Horgan, 'The Plague of Cyprian, 250-270 CE' in https://www.ancient.eu/article/992/plague-of-cyprian-250-270-ce/ Published December 13, 2016; Accessed on May 5, 2020.
[14] Ibid.
[15] 'Plague' in *World Health Organization*: https://www.who.int/news-room/fact-sheets/detail/plague/ Posted on October 31, 2017, Accessed on May 5, 2020.
[16] Scott W. Sunquist, 'Attentiveness: Pandemic': *Gordon Conwell Theological Seminary*: https://www.gordonconwell.edu/blog/pandemic/ Posted on March 12, 2020; Accessed on May 5, 2020.

charged by Martin Luther to courageously stand firm in faith in to offer care to those in need of it.[17] They did not fear contracting the diseases nor the risk of losing their own lives. This sent good signals to the world about Christianity and made the faith attractive to unbelievers.

The Spanish Influenza

Otherwise known as the Spanish flu lasted just about a year, from 1918 to 1919. It was a viral disease transmitted from birds to humans. Scientists are unsure of the source of the disease, but the first case was reported in a military base in Kansas, United States of America on March 11, 1918. According to Scott W. Sunquist, 'the flu infected 500 million people (about one-third of the world population). At least . . . 10% 'of them fell to the disease, totaling about 50 million people in one year.'[18] The Spanish influenza is one of the deadliest pandemics in human history. While other pandemics were regional, the Spanish influenza is the first known outbreak of global proportion recorded in modern history. The outbreak of the Spanish influenza in the 1900s came at a turning point in the history of contemporary world Christianity. This was about the time that Protestantism, Evangelicalism and Pentecostalism started gaining ground in Africa. The events that culminated in the birth of contemporary global Pentecostalism happened in Azusa Street shortly before this pandemic.

In Nigeria, the birth of Prophet Ayo Babalola in 1904 also took place before the Spanish Flu. The famous Ayo Babalola revival that took place later in the 1930s was part of the church's response to

---

[17] Lyman Stone, 'Christianity Has Been Handling Epidemics for 2000 Years.'
[18] Scott W. Sunquist, 'Attentiveness: Pandemic'.

the pandemic. Missionary efforts, the *Aladura* Movement, speaking in tongues, evangelism, faith healing, prayer and exorcism gained prominence during this period. These developments gave birth to some of the most renowned revival movements in the history of Christianity in Nigeria. Throughout history, the church never folded its hands in times of global health crises. It has always been part of the solution. The church reached those heights through the injection of unconditional love, sacrificial care, hope, matchless boldness, prayer and faith into the dying world of those days. Those actions increased the credibility of the church, especially among unbelievers. And when the church gains credibility in the public square, its opportunity to evangelise, and increase both spiritually and numerically skyrocket. How has the church in our time responded to COVID-19? Before we answer this question, let us first highlight some of the impacts of the COVID-19 lockdown on ordinary people on our streets in Africa using Nigeria as a case in point.

CHAPTER TWO

CONSPIRACY THEORIES, COVID-19 LOCKDOWN AND AVERAGE NIGERIANS

There have been so many conspiracy theories around the world with regards to COVID-19 since the outbreak of the pandemic in China. Like every other nation of the world, Nigeria has its own fair share of these theories. In Nigeria, there are many versions of the conspiracy theories, but two are the most prominent. The two views have to do with source of the pandemic and people's perceptions of the disease. Many Nigerians viewed it as an elite disease only for the wealthy and those in the corridor of power. This view was further compounded by the fact that some of the first set of people who tested positive to the disease were elites and Nigeria's top-ranking politicians. Some of them included: Mr. Abba Kyari, the Chief of

Staff to President Mohammadu Buhari; Mr. Bala Mohammed, the Governor of Bauchi State; Engineer Seyi Makinde, the Governor of Oyo State; Mallam Nasir el-Rufai, the Governor of Kaduna State; Mr. Okezie Ikpeazu, the Governor of Abia State; Mr. Rotimi Akeredolu, the Governor of Ondo State; Dr. Ifeanyi Okowo, the Governor of Delta State and his wife; and Senator Abiola Ajimobi, former Governor of Oyo State; etcetera. With the exception of Mr. Bala Mohammed and a few others, the public opinion held that these governors contracted the disease on a trip to a meeting that was held in March 2020 in Abuja.[1] Mr. Bala Mohammed made his COVID-19 status known to the public on March 23, 2020 shortly after returning from a trip to Lagos where he had been in contact with Mr. Mohammed Atiku Abubakar (son of the former Nigeria's vice president) who had tested positive to COVID-19 after returning from an international trip through Lagos. Ever since, many public officials and politicians have come down with or lost their lives to the disease. While some of the governors came out to the public about their COVID-19 statuses, the majority of them did not but were believed to have quietly gone into self-isolation. This development caused many members of the public to assume the disease came only for the rich in our society. According to a BBC report, 'The Nigeria Centre for Disease Control has recorded more than 600 cases since the end of February – most of them people who had been abroad, and those they had interacted with upon their return to Nigeria.'[2] Meanwhile, most Nigerians view

---

[1] Tofe Ayeni, 'Coronavirus: Nigeria's Varied Responses to Controlling COVID-19' in *theafricareport*: https://www.theafricareport.com/27773/coronaviru-nigerias-varied-responses-to-controlling-covid-19/ Posted May 13, 2020, Accessed on June 2, 2020.

[2] 'Coronavirus: Why Some Nigerians are Gloating About COVID-19' in *BBC*: https://www.bbc.com/news/world-africa-52372737/ Posted on April 23, 2020, Accessed on June 1, 2020.

anyone who travels abroad as privileged and rich. This perception was partly why the efforts of the government to contain the spread of the disease became more difficult.

The worst came on the April 17, 2020 when Mr. Abba Kyari died as a result of COVID-19 complications. Public opinion held that the fall of Mr. Abba Kyari to COVID-19 was from God, and that it was a signal to corrupt politicians who failed to invest in the country's healthcare system before the outbreak of the pandemic. According to BBC:

> Nigerians spent more than $1bn on treatment in overseas hospitals in 2013. President Buhari promised to end "medical tourism" when they took power in 2015, but he himself spent more than four months in London in 2017 getting treatment for an undisclosed illness and subsequently returning to the UK capital for additional care. But with borders closed and each country haunted by its own COVID-19 nightmare, Nigeria's big men and women are now forced to use their country's hospitals, prompting many a stream of taunts and jokes.[3]

Even the Secretary to the Federation, Mr. Boss Mustapha was on record for publicly admitting that he did not know that the Nigeria's health sector was in such a deplorable state until he was made the Chairman of the Presidential Task Force on COVID-19.[4] He and other public leaders were criticised for their insensitive

---

[3] Ibid.
[4] Tessy Igomu, 'I didn't Know Nigeria's Health Sector was this Bad' in *Punch HealthWise*: https://healthwise.punch.com/i-did-know-nigerias-health-sector-was-this-bad-boss-mustapha/ Posted on April 10, 2020, Accessed on June 1, 2020.

medical trips abroad to the detriment of the country's health sector. Many Nigerians concluded that the COVID-19 disease was God's punishment for the Nigerian elite and politicians for not putting the interest of the country at heart. Senators Adebayo Oshinowo and Abiola Ajimobi are few out of notable Nigerian politicians who have died as a result of COVID-19 complications, after the demise of Abba Kyari.

Besides the above, there were those who erroneously tied the COVID-19 disease to the 5G expansion. Adherents of this view argued that the disease stemmed out of the electromagnetic radiation emitting from the fifth generation telecommunication network expansion in Nigeria. Prince Osuagwu records that, 'The claims are that the virus started in a 5G smart city in China and was reported that the first case happened exactly the day mandatory vaccines started in the country. According to the claim, the vaccine contained replicating digitized Ribonucleic acid (RNA), which was activated by 60Ghz waves that were turned on in Wuhan, as well as other countries using 60Ghz 5G, and that incidentally, the acid created smart dust that everyone on the globe has been inhaling through chemtrails.'[5] This conspiracy theory made the rounds on the Nigeria's social media for some time and also made the fight against COVID-19 difficult, this time among the elites.

There was also a theological dimension to the matter. The perceptions highlighted earlier were further reinforced by the theological perceptions of some evangelical leaders in the country on the COVID-19 disease. Notable among these leaders were Pastor Christ Oyakhilome, the President of Believers Love World, also known as Christ Embassy and Bishop David Oyedepo, founder of

---

[5] Prince Osuagwu, 'Nigeria: COVID-19, 5G Mix-Up – Why Nigerians are Worried' in *allAfrica:* https://allafrica.com/stories/202004080125.html/ Posted on April 8, 2020, Accessed on June 1, 2020.

the Living Faith Church, also known as Winner's Chapel and one the largest evangelical megachurches in Nigeria. Oyakhilome linked the coronavirus pandemic and 5G network to the biblical antichrist and part of the signs of the end of times.[6] Bishop David Oyedepo was arguably the most audible voice among the evangelicals against government restrictions on religious gathering. In his words, "The church is God's banquet hall where we are fed with spiritual food to keep us alive and strong. So whatever stops the church from fellowshipping is out to destroy what God is building... There must be a devil behind it. It is not a virus; it is a demon. There is a demon at work behind the scene. I told you in the morning, I smell a rat."[7]

Both Oyakhilome and Oyedepo's views have three implications. Firstly, they suggest that COVID-19 is not natural. Rather, it is a man-made disease that is traceable to the 5G network. Secondly, they imply that the closure of churches is tantamount to crippling the Christian faith or exterminating the spiritual lives of Christians. Thirdly, they submit that Satan is responsible for the outbreak of COVID-19 in the world and that it has eschatological implications. Experts claim that COVID-19 has nothing to do with 5G. In spite of all the attempts made by the authorities of the Nigerian Communication Commission (NCC) to debunk the 5G myth, many members of the public held tight to the views expressed by these prominent evangelical leaders on the

---

[6] Pastor Chris, '5G is Lovely But' in https://youtu.be/lXnLwtAS6Fk/ Posted on April 8, 2020. See also Mayowa Kwushue, 'Coronavirus: Pastor Chris Makes Fearful Revelations about the COVID-19, New Vaccine, and Antichrist' in *Nigeria News World*: https://nigerianewsworld.com/news/coronavirus-pastor-chris-makes-fearful-revelations-about-covid-19-new-vaccine-5g-antichrist-video/ Posted on April 5, 2020, Accessed on June 1, 2020.

[7] Christian Kripphl, 'Nigerian Religious Leaders Demand Lifting of COVID-19 Lockdown' in *DW*: https://m.dw.com/en/nigerian-religious-leaders-demand-lifting-of-covid-19-lockdown/a-53499533/ Posted on May 5, 2020, Accessed on June 2, 2020.

disease. Both Oyakhilome and Oyedepo have millions of followers across the world, and one can only imagine the impact of their views on those followers. While telecommunication experts may be able to dissuade many from following this view on COVID-19 and 5G, very little can be achieved when it comes to the impact of Oyakhilome and Oyedepo's theological influence on their mammoth admirers across the world. Meanwhile, in the Muslim Hausa community, there is a fatalistic attitude and a refusal among the *talakawa* to take any precautions. These perceptions affected the general response of the public to the disease.

Obviously, many Nigerian Christians believe in these conspiracy theories being floated across the country, and sadly, this is against the teaching of the Bible. Daniel Gachuki warns that "Christians would be naïve to think that conspiracy theories have no consequences."[8] He stresses further: 'Conspiracy theories were a potent tool in the hands of Emperor Nero as he sought to exterminate early Christians. Adolf Hitler used them to incite hatred against the Jews. And Satan also used it to turn Adam and Even against God in the Garden of Eden (Genesis 3).'[9] The Bible warns Christians against making wrong claims or propaganda and spreading falsehood (Exodus 23:1, 1 Thessalonians 5:21).

COVID-19 LOCKDOWN AND AVERAGE NIGERIANS

What are the socio-economic effects of COVID-19 lockdown on average Nigerians? Aside from the religious implications of

---

[8] Daniel Gachuki, '3 Reasons Not to Support Conspiracy Theories' in *The Gospel Coalition Africa*: https://africa.thegospelcoalition.org/article/why-you-shouldnt-support-conspiracy-theories/ Posted on May 12, 2020, Accessed on June 1, 2020.
[9] Ibid.

the novel COVID-19 pandemic due to the lockdown order by the Federal Government of Nigeria, as in many countries of the world, its socio-economic impacts now and in the future cannot be underestimated. A few of these consequences include: anti-social behaviour, loss of job/sources of income, increase in unemployment rate, increase in family size, change in lifestyle, insecurity, hunger, disruptions of educational activities and inflation, among others.

Anti-Social Behaviour

People exhibit antisocial behaviour when they behave differently from the acceptable standard that guides the daily conduct of members in a society. Antisocial behaviour is any action or behaviour that violates the social and cultural norms of a particular group of people in the society.[10] In this period of lockdown when immobility is taking tolls on the living pattern of Nigerian citizens, especially those who eke out a living from daily business activities, many young people, for instance, may try to take advantage of the situation to indulge in antisocial behaviour, including: burglary, sexual abuse, internet fraud, prostitution, assault, rape and suicide, among others. Many hands that are not doing anything meaningful or involved in legitimate business are likely to engage in this behaviour. For instance, the incumbent Inspector General of Police reported at a press briefing by the Presidential Task Force on COVID-19 on Friday, April 24, 2020 on the NTA at 9:00PM that during this lockdown period, innocent citizens are being attacked and deprived of their properties, especially in Lagos and the Ogun States of Nigeria. In the same vein, news was circulating that a robbery gang, tagged,

---

[10] Isaac Otumala, *Rudiments of Sociology* (Lagos: Sunkorin Enterprises, 2013), 112.

1 million Boys, had terrorized Lagos residents in the midst of this stay-at-home order.

Loss of Jobs/Sources of Income

It is no longer news that most shops and offices have closed in Nigeria, especially in the urban centres, with only the essential ones remaining open. Many people, as a result of this lockdown, may have lost their sources of income. For instance, a large majority of artisans, those doing menial jobs and making a living out of *Okada* (commercial motorcycle) riding business are out of job and with no adequate provision for their welfare; even though, the Federal Government of Nigeria is said to have been distributing palliatives to some vulnerable people in the country, the majority are still disappointed because it has not reached them. Some may, however, resort to sharp practices to make a living in a time as this. Those who are in the private sectors are likely to lose their jobs due to lack of production and inability to render services. It is not out of point to find that many private workers have not received their March salaries due to the lockdown. This threatened their means of livelihood with resultant inability to meet basic needs, such as health care, electricity and rent payment. It is interesting to note that the post-COVID-19 pandemic may likely pose a difficult time for employees. Keeping their jobs may become an uphill task because there are no guarantees for job security. Many organisations may contemplate laying off workers in order to keep afloat.

At the institutional level, the temporary closing down of revenue generating services, such as airports, waterways, as well as manufacturing industries and the like would result in a decline in internally generated income with attendant consequences on government expenditures at all levels.

Increase in unemployment

Unemployment is a universal social and economic problem. Every country of the world, both advanced and developing, is grappling with it. In this part of the world, the baseline trend of unemployment before the pandemic was already alarming; with the devastating consequences of the COVID-19 pandemic, those without work, those currently available for work, and those seeking work are going to be hard hit. The rate of unemployment is likely to significantly increase in Nigeria. As a result of the fall-out from the pandemic, many people may lose their jobs, especially in the private sector, and governments at all levels are not likely to employ more people due to the decrease in oil prices and low production which has already affected the 2020 budget.

Akanni and Gabriel assert that the slowdown in the global economy and lockdown in most countries, including Nigeria, as a result of the COVID-19 pandemic has taken its toll on the global demand for oil, coupled with the logjam between Russia and the OPEC Cartel on the decision to cut output.[11] It is, however, sad to state that the picture of the future economy in Nigeria has been painted bleak by the International Monetary Fund (IMF). It projected that Nigeria was heading into its worst recession in over thirty years and that 20 million Nigerians may lose jobs (Nigerian Tribune, 2020).[12] This was also supported by Damilola Akinbami who opined that

---

[11] Lateef Olawale Akanni, and Samuel Chukwudi Gabriel, 'Of COVID-19 Pandemic on the Nigerian Economy' in *Centre for the Study of the Economies of Africa (CSEA)*: http://cseaafrica.org/the-implication-of-covid19-on-the-nigerian-economy/ Accessed on April 29, 2020.

[12] Chima Nwokoji, 'IMF Projects Negative GDP Growth for Nigeria in 2020' in *Nigerian Tribune Newspaper*: https://tribuneonlineng.com/imf-projects-negative-gdp-growth-for-nigeria-in-2020/ Posted on April 14, 2020, Accessed on April 29, 2020.

analysts have argued that Nigeria's economy is likely to head for a recession by the end of the year 2020 due to the massive decline in crude oil prices caused by the coronavirus pandemic, and this lead to further devaluation with its attendant consequences, including a high rate of unemployment.[13]

Increase in family size

In Nigeria, with a population of over 200 million people, increase in family size due to the lockdown order by the government as a result of COVID-19 is imminent, and this can grossly add to the existing high rate of population growth. The stay-at-home order would afford couples time to interact sexually with each other more than before, and this may result in many wanted and unwanted pregnancies. The implication is that the total number of births per woman would likely increase. That is, more children would be birthed after the COVID-19 episode if couples do not utilize contraceptive methods and devices, and this may have adverse effects on the low-income earners as they have to feed more mouths than their income.

Insecurity

One other difficulty that may arise as a result of this pandemic is insecurity. The phenomenon of insecurity presents a significant challenge to the citizens of Nigeria. In recent times, Boko Haram insurgency, kidnapping, ethno-religious crises, herder-farmer feuds and banditry, among others, have been a source of insecurity

---

[13] Damilola Akinbami, How Can Nigeria Withstand the Economic Impact of COVID-19? In *Africa Business News,* April 12, 2020.

challenges that are threatening the existence of Nigeria as a political entity. Little did we know that the security of the nation would be challenged by a greater enemy, an armless organism, called coronavirus in the beginning of this year.

Citing Jatau and Kumnah, Acumba, Ighomereho and Akpor-Robaro, "Insecurity is lack of safety, exposure to danger, hazard, uncertainty, and want of confidence, state of doubt, instability, trouble, lack of protection, and being unsafe."[14] Insecurity appears to be the greatest threat in the current global health crisis. COVID -19, especially in Nigeria, has affected the attitude, confidence, social aspects and the emotional health of households. The cherished values, including free movement, interaction with kith and kin and the survival of individuals and groups are being threatened. It is clear that this pandemic has exposed Nigerian citizens to a form of insecurity that, if nothing is urgently changed about the lockdown order, may lead to non-conformity and its resultant chaos in many communities due to the total lockdown being alien to them.

Change in lifestyle

The self-isolation and social distancing being executed by the government in Nigeria due to COVID -19 pandemic, would continue to affect the behaviour of many Nigerians in numerous ways, both positively and negatively. From the positive dimension, it is interesting to note that due to work and business commitments, many couples as well as family members hardly stayed together as

---

[14] Audu Andrew Jatau, and Banmang Kumnah, 'Factors Associated with Internal Insecurity and the Impact on the Health of Families in Nigeria', *Nigerian Journal of Health Education*, Vol. 19 (1), 23. (21-35).

much as during the lockdown when movements were restricted. This afforded many the opportunity to re-enact their long-lost love and affection due to lack of sufficient time and stressful activities.

Since the outbreak of the pandemic, several preventive measures have been rolled out by governments in different countries with recommendations from health organisations, including the World Health Organisation, to curtail the community spread of the pandemic. Some of these preventive measures include, among others: social and physical distancing, hand-washing and hygiene practices, wearing face masks and lockdown. These practices have really affected the way we do things in Nigeria. This is not unconnected to the level of awareness about the pandemic; although, some are still showing lackadaisical attitude to the infection. It is not out of point to state that, even after the end of this pandemic, some of these practices, especially hand-washing may become part of our daily hygiene habits.

It is also instructive to state that more people are likely to indulge in alcohol consumption while staying at home. This is evident in a study among three thousand workers in the United States conducted by the American Addiction Centers Resource in which about one-third of the participants agreed to drinking while working from home during the COVID-19 pandemic and one-fifth stockpiled alcohol for self-isolation.[15] This suggests that during this period, since many people are inside doing little or nothing, they are likely to recline with bottles of alcohol.

---

[15] American Addiction Resource Centers (2020) 'Drinking Alcohol While Working from Home' in *Alcohol.org: An American Centers Resources Alcohol Consumption:* https://www.alcohol.org/guides/work-from-home-drinking/ 2020, Accessed on April 29, 2020.

Hunger

There is also the problem of hunger and ill health associated with the COVID-19 pandemic in Nigeria. Many Nigerians live from hand to mouth; when people who make their living on daily basis, such as artisans, petty traders, commercial motorcycle riders (Okada riders), street hawkers, and a host of others, are shut-in for too long, there is the tendency for them to go hungry, and this may have some devastating effects on their wellness. No wonder, many have insinuated that the "hunger virus" is more deadly than coronavirus. In fact, in a survey conducted by NOI-Polls (2020), 72 % of the respondents were concerned about the lockdown, mainly due to hunger associated with the high cost and lack of food for the poor since their daily sources of livelihood have been placed on hold due to the COVID-19 pandemic.[16]

Disruptions of Educational activities

It is a known fact that education is the major pillar of any nation's socio-economic and political development, and that no nation can rise above the quality of her education. Thus, the role of education, in all ramifications in the life of individuals and the nation, cannot be underestimated. However, Nigeria, like any other developing country before the COVID-19 pandemic, had been grappling with a myriad of problems associated with its educational system including: poor or inadequate funding, inadequate infrastructural facilities, manpower needs, and overpopulation of students, poverty, corruption and value

---

[16] NOI-Polls 'COVID-19 Poll Result Release' in https://noi-polls.com/covid-19-poll-result-release/ Posted on March 18, 2020 and Accessed on April 29, 2020.

disintegration.[17] With the outbreak of the COVID-19 pandemic, Nigeria's educational sector has taken its share of the challenge.

The decision to close educational institutions and schools across the globe since March 2020 in an attempt to contain the spread of the pandemic has also led to a soaring number of children, youth and adults not attending schools.[18] Quoting the UNESCO Monitoring Report on COVID-19 Educational Disruptions and Response, 'the impact of school closures in the over 100 countries that have implemented the decisions around the world has impacted over half of the global students' population.'[19] The ripple effects of these closures cannot be underestimated. For instance, in a systematic review to know whether school measures are effective in the coronavirus outbreak by Russell Viner and others, they noted the adverse effects of the school closures to include: economic harms to working parents, healthcare workers and other key workers being forced from work to childcare and to society due to loss of parental productivity, loss of education, harm to child welfare, particularly, and nutritional problems, especially to children for whom school meals are an important source of nutrition.[20] The authors stated that, according to figures from UNESCO, these school closures have affected more than 1.5 billion children and young people.[21]

---

[17] Michael Olamide Ogunyemi, *Problems and Challenges facing Higher Education Management in Nigeria: A Sociological and Philosophical Perspective* (Port Harcourt: Thaworld Global Resources Limited, 2003), 22.
[18] Lateef Olawale Akanni, and Samuel Chukwudi Gabriel.
[19] Ibid.
[20] Russell M. Viner, Simon J. Russell, Helen Croker, et al (2020) 'School Closure and Management Practices during Coronavirus Outbreaks including COVID-19: A Rapid Systematic Review' in *The Lancet Child and Adolescent Health Journal*, Vol.4, Issue 5 (May 01, 2020) Published on April 6, 2020: https://www.thelancet.com/journals/lanchi/article/PIIS2352-4642(20)30095-X/fulltext/ 397-404, Accessed on April 29, 2020.
[21] Ibid.

Thus, it is only fair to agree that the education sector has suffered the most. Since the suspension of all teaching and learning activities in the country, students have been spending time at home, with no idea of when to go back to school. In an attempt to provide intervention measures, the Federal Government of Nigeria has ordered that learning should be done online in the interim pending the end of the pandemic cases in Nigeria, especially with a view to assisting in the continued running of academic programmes.

Inflation

The continued lockdown of Nigerians in their various houses may bring about an increase in the rate of inflation. This is because, before the lockdown, many people who had the financial ability to were able to stockpile food items and other basic needs. However, if this persisted, many households would run out of stock, and if the sellers are unable to move out to buy and stock their stores, there may be inflation because there would be more demand than supplies. At present, many Nigerians are already using the current situation to make money by hiking the prices of goods and services, including food stuffs and other consumables. Even in states where there are no total lockdowns, the cost of transportation has also increased.

Health Crises

While the Coronavirus lockdown was by itself a response to a global health crisis, that development came with tendencies that could further complicate the health of many Nigerians. These complications came in at least three ways: obesity, accessibility to medical facilities and health care providers and high cost of medical services. The inactivity and redundancy occasioned by the coronavirus lockdown have caused many to add to their body weight mass. This was particularly the case with those who had enough to eat but had little to do. Therefore, the lockdown made them prone to other medical complications associated with being overweight. In addition to this was the difficulty in accessing health workers and medical facilities. In a country suffering from acute shortage of healthcare practitioners and poor healthcare facilities, one can only imagine the stress that the coronavirus pandemic would put on the already overwhelmed health sector.

As of 2019, Nigeria had about 42,000 medical doctors to a population of over 200 million people. In the words of the president of the Nigeria Medical Association (NMA), Dr. Franscis Faduyile, 'there are 75,000 Nigerian doctors registered with the body but over 33,000 have left the country, leaving behind only about 42,000 to all health institutions in the country.'[22] He stresses further that 'In rural areas, we have one doctor to 22,000 people, while in towns and cities, we have one doctor to 10,000 to 12,000 Nigerians.'[23] To worsen the matter, a significant number of these healthcare workers leave Nigeria for greener pastures abroad due to insecurity, low remunerations, a poor health system and other basic infrastructures. Meanwhile, the ideal ration prescribed by the World Health Organization is one doctor to six hundred people. Clearly, the system was already overwhelmed even before the lockdown. There were reports of some health workers absconding from their duties or having to turn down patients of other forms of illnesses during the lockdown, due to the fear of being exposed to possible coronavirus cases. The poor

---

[22] Martins Ifijeh, 'Nigeria Has Only 42,000 Doctors to 200 Million People, NMA President Cries Out' in *AllAfrica*: https://allafrica.com/stories/201912190053.html/ Posted on December 19, 2020; Accessed on May 2, 2020.
[23] Ibid.

management of the health sector by the Nigerian government has made it difficult to blame any doctor for failing to effectively perform his or her duties. It goes without saying how stressful and financially burdensome it would be for vulnerable Nigerians to access and pay for health services during the lockdown.

CHAPTER THREE
EVANGELICAL CHRISTIANITY IN AFRICA

What is Evangelical Christianity and how was it being practiced, especially in Africa, before the outbreak of coronavirus? Evangelicalism is a dynamic force and one of the most influential Christian traditions in the world today. From the onset of Evangelicalism in Great Britain in the 1730s to the United States in the nineteenth century, and now as a global phenomenon, evangelicals have had great influence in many spheres of human life and society. Throughout the twentieth century, a series of gatherings and movements converged into the Lausanne Movement and the World Evangelical Alliance (WEA), arguably the two most active global bodies of Evangelicals today.[1] The

---

[1] 'Number of Evangelicals worldwide' in *Lausanne Movement* on https://www.lausanne.org/lgc-transfer/number-of-evangelicals-worldwide, Accessed on June 22, 2019.

Association of Evangelicals in Africa (AEA), a member of WEA, is the largest evangelical umbrella body on the African continent. The growth of the evangelical movement in the last half-century has been quite phenomenal. A recent survey reveals that there are about 700 million evangelicals in the world today. This implies that one out of every four Christians is an evangelical.[2] Their success is largely traceable to the quality and impact of evangelical spirituality, as well as its rootedness in the Word of God.

Evangelicals can be categorized into two dominant configurations. First, they are a movement of Christians persuaded by certain doctrinal convictions and practices. As such, they can be found in virtually any Christian tradition, be it Protestant, Anglican, Roman Catholic, Orthodox, Pentecostal, Charismatic or Independent. Secondly, evangelicals are Christian denominations established and administered on evangelical ethos. However, the seemingly fluid configuration of evangelicalism in the West is not the case in Africa. In Africa, doctrinal and liturgical differences have mounted thick demarcations between denominations that would have been naturally classified as evangelicals in the West. For example, the Africa Inland Church (AIC), Baptists, Deeper Life Bible Church, Evangelical Church Winning All (ECWA), United Missionary Church of Africa (UMCA), Church of Christ in Nations (COCIN), Redeemed Christian Church of God (RCCG), Foursquare Gospel Church in Nigeria (FGCN), Christ Is the Answer Ministries (CITAM) and The Assemblies of God (AoG), to mention just a few, would all have been classified as evangelicals in the West. But that is not the case in Africa. These factors have been largely responsible for the prevalence of schism and mushrooming of churches and sectionalism within the African

---

[2] 'Number of Evangelicals worldwide.'

Christian tapestry. Specific attention is given to the relationship between the Evangelical and Pentecostal-Charismatic Christianity in Africa in the next chapter.

The African Church versus the Church in Africa

Permit me to raise an observation here before we delve into the heart of our concern in this chapter. The observation borders on making a choice between *the African Church* and *the Church in Africa*. For the purpose of this study, the phrase *African Church* or the *church in Africa* are used interchangeably in this book. Two factors are responsible for this proposition. Firstly, my initial concern borders on geography. Whereas the intention of the topic is to focus on the Church in Africa, the phrase *African Church* suggests the inclusion of the African church in diaspora, which is outside the scope and focus of this particular book. Secondly, I will like to add my voice to the ongoing scholarly discourse on whether or not it is proper and biblical to use the phrase *African Church* or *African Christianity*. Those against the use of these terms have argued that they promote ethnicity, schism, sectionalism and cultural differences in the *ecclesia* of Christ, which they submit, are against the precepts of the Holy Bible.[3] On the contrary, the term *African Church* is primarily concerned with composition and location. That is, the church in Africa and the diaspora, with Africans as its predominant attendees. *African Christianity*, on the other hand, is the brand of Christian

---

[3] Olusegun Adeniyi, '"You are the Light of the World": The Church in the Public Eye.' The Third Vitality Lecture Delivered at the Centre for Biblical Christianity in Africa on Friday, June 7, 2019: 2-4. See also Conrad Mbewe, 'Why There is no such Thing as African Christianity' in https://www.9marks.org/article/why-theres-no-such-thing-as-african-christianity/Accessed on June 24, 2019.

faith that is expressed within the African socio-cultural milieu and other realities that are uniquely African.

In his book, *The Missionary Movement in Christian History*, Andrew Walls introduces two principles that explain the relationship between the gospel and culture and how that has influenced the growth of Christianity throughout history. These principles are the *indigenizing principle* and the *pilgrim principle*. Walls argues that through the history of the Church, starting from the first place of its origin, Palestine, Christianity has always been a faith that has continuity in all places it finds itself.[4] The basic elements of this continuity according to Walls are the significant places that Jesus maintains in the faith in all cultures, the sense of continuity that Christianity has even in cultures outside Palestine, and the continuity of the sacrament of holy communion (bread and wine) and baptism (water) as well as the belief in and the use of one Bible in all cultures.[5] According to Walls, the *continuity* reality of the gospel is also the cause of the opposing tendencies in the transmission of the Christian faith–the *indigenizing principle* and the *pilgrim principle*.[6]

Walls explains that, while the ultimate purpose of the Christian faith and expansion is transformation, the Gospel does not deal with people in isolation of the cultural contexts they belong to and the relationships they have. In fact, he contends that it is impossible to completely separate people from their cultural orientations and social relationships, even when they accept the Gospel.[7] He adds that this is so because Christ accepts believers as they are within their

---

[4] Andrew Walls, *The Missionary Movement in Christian History: Studies in the Transmission of Faith* (Maryknoll, New York: Orbis Books, 1996), 6.

[5] Ibid.

[6] Ibid.

[7] Walls, *The Missionary Movement in Christian History*, 6.

cultural milieu. The process of being a Christian and yet remaining true to one's culture, context and social relationships is what he describes as the indigenizing principle. In other words, the gospel is being indigenized or incorporated into the receptor's context and everyday life.

He argues that this tendency has been a significant factor behind the expansion and transmission of the Christian faith through history.[8] This implies that people are able to express their Christian faith while their social and cultural consciousnesses are intact. Through history, the Christian faith and its associated theologies are culturally conditioned irrespective of where they are found. The indigenizing principle partly explains the shift of the heartlands of Christianity from the Global North to South and also shows that the development of Christian theology depends on the interaction of the Gospel within cultures.

The questions that follow Walls' indigenizing principle therefore are: Is every aspect of the human culture compatible with the gospel? Are Christians to practice every aspect of their culture, even when they are contrary to the gospel? The process of isolating the incompatible aspects of culture with the gospel is the other force in tension with the indigenizing principle–the pilgrim principle.[9] Walls through the pilgrim principle contends that, while culture is very important, Christians must also allow the gospel to transform their minds and cultures. Christians, irrespective of their nationality, enjoy adoptive privilege as part of the history of Israel and are part of a new family through Christ. Therefore, Christians are on a pilgrimage towards Christlikeness. The pilgrim principle implies that Christians must know that, although they live in this world, the

---

[8] Ibid., 7-8.
[9] Ibid., 7-8.

world is not their ultimate home. So, they must strive to reject aspects of their cultures that contradict the gospel.

The indigenizing and pilgrim principles help to partly explain that theology is born out of practical situations emerging from traceable historical events. Theology develops as the Christian gospel seeks to respond to the challenges of cultural realities and the sociopolitical contexts in which it finds itself.[10] Walls describes the transmission of the gospel in the contemporary world Christianity as the *Ephesian Movement*. Just as it was with the Church at Ephesus, the modern church is a movement where every member of the body of Christ, irrespective of race, gender, culture and nationality, executes their gifts for the growth of the world church.[11] Under this new world church reality, there are no superior people and there is no epicenter it is every member of the body of Christ playing their part. The diverse expressions of Christian faith, rooted in indigenous worldview and cultural practices, helps to provide a theological and missiological understanding on the shift in the heartlands of Christianity from the Northern Hemisphere to the Global South and East.

Therefore, against the promotion of ethnicity and sectionalism, the term *African Church* is about the dominant composition of church attendees, while that of *African Christianity* is about how Africans express *their* Christianity, as well as how that expression can add value to the expression of Christianity globally. This expression can only be authentic when it is in conformity with the Word of God. This is the spirit behind the publishing of the Africa Study Bible and Africa Bible Commentary.

---

[10] Walls, *The Missionary Movement in Christian History,* 10-11.

[11] Andrew Walls, *The Cross-Cultural Process in Christian History* (Maryknoll, New York: Orbis Books, 2002).

Evangelical Identity and Spirituality

The terms *evangelicalism* and *evangelical(s)* are non-static. They are fluid terms going through different reconstructions at different stages of church growth and history. It is, therefore, essential that we review the meaning of the terms again, at least for the purpose of operationalizing them in this book. David Lumsdaine explains that 'The word "Evangelicalism" is used in a wide variety of ways. British Anglicans use the term to refer to the kind of liturgy that is celebrated on Sunday. Many elites in the United States use the term as a polite substitute for "fundamentalism" and considered it unreasonable, militant, backward and uneducated Protestantism.'[12] Due to the diversities of these perspectives, there are many within our context who have been practicing the Evangelical brand of Christianity for years but who do not possess the requisite knowledge to defend their identity and beliefs when the need arises. This is an identity crisis that should not be left unattended. The first step necessary to thrive in our Christian living is to be sure of our identity in Christ.

Evangelicalism is the aspect of the Christian faith that emphasizes the good news of the gospel of Jesus Christ, literally the *evangel*, which is proclaimed as an invitation to whoever believes and receives it. It is a personal encounter with God through Christ that leads to the transformation and renewal of the lives of its recipients. This could be seen as a universal definition of Evangelicalism. There are four key concepts in this definition which are: *good news, proclamation, personal encounter* and *transformation*. To take away any one of

---

[12] David H. Lumsdaine, 'Evangelical Christianity and Democratic Pluralism in Asia: An Introduction' in *Evangelical Christianity and Democracy in Asia*, David Halloran Lumsdaine, ed., (Oxford: Oxford University Press, 2009), 7.

these concepts is to have something less than Evangelicalism.[13] The famous *Bebbington quadrilateral*, describes these four characteristics as: crucicentrism, conversionism, Biblicalism, and activism.[14] Evangelicals are affiliated church members who adhere to these four cardinal qualities. This generally means they have grounded belief in the crucified Christ, an experience of a personal conversion (being *born-again*), theological foundation on the Bible as the infallible Word of God and an active missionary evangelism or preaching of the Gospel.

In a more recent definition, former president of the National Association of Evangelicals (NAE) in the United States, Ted Haggard submits that "An evangelical is a Christian believer who: (1) believes that Jesus Christ is the Son of God, (2) believes the Bible is the Word of God, (3) believes in the necessity of being born again."[15] Haggard did not add Evangelism in his definition as did David Bebbington. Like Bebbington, I consider evangelism to be central to the evangelical identity, and so, I will equally consider it in our discussion.

There are central issues in the definitions above. I would like to take a departure from Ted Haggard's definition of evangelicals. Firstly, note the use of article *the* in the Christological aspect of the definition. That is to say, Jesus is *the* Son and not *a* son of God. That makes a considerable difference. This is the very heart of evangelical Christianity, spirituality, worldview and practice. That singular fact

---

[13] A.O. Balcomb, 'Evangelicalism in Africa: What it is and What it Does' in *Southern African Journal of Missiology: Missionalia* (Online), Vol. 44, No 2, (Pretoria 2016): http://www.scielo.org.za/scielo.php?script=sci_arttext&pid=S0256-95072016000200002, Cited on Tuesday 18 June, 2019.

[14] D.W. Bebbington, *Evangelicalism in Modern Britain: A History from the 1730s to the 1980s* (Oxfordshire: Routledge, 1989), 20.

[15] Ted Haggard, *Your Primary Purpose: How to reach your Community and World for Christ* (Lake Mary: Florida, 2006), 36.

changes everything. It changes our response to modernism and postmodernism and our theologizing on Christology, Soteriology, Hamartiology, Ecclesiology and Eschatology, to mention a few. In missiology, it changes how we reflect on the subjects of conversion, incarnation, contextualization, indigenization, acculturation, adaption, accommodation and translation.

This same factor changes our response as evangelicals to religious pluralism and exclusivism, to syncretism and dialoguing with people of other faiths. For instance, what is the ultimate purpose of dialogue? If the primary concern of religious dialogue is about how people of different faiths could co-exist and cohabit peacefully, then, at what point do Christians fulfill the Matthew 28:18–20 mandate? Should they verbalize their evangelization or just flesh it out in their conducts, or both? Where is the limit of dialogue with people of other faiths for evangelical Christians?

Besides, knowing that Jesus is *the* Son and not *a* son of God should change our response to what I refer to as the *transactional Christianity* that is common at present, especially within the African Christian milieu and tapestry. *Transactional Christianity* is when a *Christian* worships primarily because of the benefits that will be derived from God and not essentially because God deserves unconditional worship. Evangelicals believe that the work of Jesus on the cross, his death and resurrection are the only source of salvation and forgiveness of sins. They believe that salvation comes not by works but through faith in Jesus Christ alone. People can do nothing to earn their way to heaven. Instead, believers do good works in grateful response to their pardon, not to cause it.[16] Therefore, Evangelical Christians have an unconditional duty and mission to

---

[16] Traci Schumacher, '5 Beliefs that Sets Evangelical Apart from other Christians' in https://www.newsmax.com/fastfeatures/evangelical-christians-beliefs/2015/04/02/id/636050/ Posted April 2, 2015.

emulate and promote the person, life and ministry of Jesus Christ as God's standard for fulfilling our mission on earth whether as an individual, family or *ecclesia*.

Secondly, another important issue to illuminate in the definitions (of *evangelicals*) above is the authority of the Word of God. The Word of God is central to the evangelical spirituality, theology and practice. In the words of Stanley Grenz, "Evangelicals boldly maintain that the primary focus of the divine self-disclosure is Jesus Christ and that the Bible is the deposit of the divine revelation in history."[17] Without doubt, the Bible is crucial to the evangelical project.[18] Mark Noll, a foremost American historian corroborates that:

> When examining the evangelical study of Scripture, everything hinges upon recognition that the evangelical community considers the Bible the very Word of God . . . Although evangelicals typically give some attention to the human character of the Bible, they believe that Scripture itself teaches that where the Bible speaks, God speaks.[19]

This is certainly the pillar which the *inerrancy* of the Word of God, a cardinal tenet Evangelicals hang upon. While it is not the concern of this book, I must mention for our education that evangelicals have often been criticized by scholars with critical approaches to exegesis for being too defensive of the Bible.[20] I am persuaded that

---

[17] Stanley J. Grenz, *Revisioning Evangelical Theology: A Fresh Agenda for the 21st Century* (Downers Groves, Illinois, 1993), 111.
[18] Grenz, *Revisioning Evangelical Theology*, 111.
[19] Mark A. Noll, *Between Faith and Criticism: Evangelical, Scholarship and the Bible in America* (San Francisco: Harper & Row, 1986), 6.
[20] Grenz, 110.

these scientific criticisms are unwarranted. "Evangelical spirituality views the Bible as the place–ultimately the only place–to go to find the words of everlasting life. As evangelicals, we believe the Bible is, in Clark Pinnock's description of the phenomenon, "the God-given documentation which preserves for all time the Gospel of our salvation. Consequently, ordinary believers know instinctively from the Spirit, their teacher, to go there to be nourished in their faith."[21] So, the evangelical commitment to the Bible is crucial, for Scripture forms the foundation for the evangelical ethos and agenda.

If at the heart of evangelicalism rests our common vision of the nature of being Christian and if this vision is linked to the nature of the stories of our *experience with the Lord,* then the Bible is significant. The Scriptures provide the categories by which we can understand ourselves and organize our narratives. In short, from the message of the Bible we gain our identity as the people of God. And through the Bible we learn what it means to be the community of faith on earth.[22] Evangelicals believe that the absolutes of Scripture are what the world needs now more than ever, hence, its emphasis on the teaching and preaching ministry of the church and the training of pastoral trainers and practitioners.

Therefore, Evangelicals believe in the Bible as God's inspired Word to humankind, perfect in truth in the original text. It is the final authority in all matters of doctrine and faith and above all human authority.[23] However, it is not enough to idolize the Bible

---

[21] Grenz, 111. See also Clark H. Pinnock, 'What Is Biblical Inerrancy?' in *Proceedings of the Conference on Biblical Inerrancy 1987* (Nashville: Broadman, 1987), 75.

[22] Grenz, 135-6.

[23] Traci Schumacher, '5 Beliefs that Sets Evangelical Apart from other Christians' in https://www.newsmax.com/fastfeatures/evangelical-christians-beliefs/2015/04/02/id/636050/ Posted April 2, 2015.

as we are being accused by some *non-evangelicals*. We must show commitment to obeying and living by the instructions given to us by God in the pages of Scripture.

The third pillar is personal salvation. Being born-again is the key that unlocks an eternal relationship with God. It is the beginning of our spiritual walk with and works for God. It is a non-negotiable experience that every Christian must have. According to Stanley Grenz:

> The pietistic impulse maintains that a personal *experience* is foundational to the Christian life. Conversion is the irreplaceable, non-negotiable beginning point of the believer's walk with the Lord, which in turn is the pathway of spirituality. As a result of this central interest, we continually ask, "Are you born again? Have you experienced the transforming power of Christ?" The new birth, however, is but the beginning of experiential religion. Conversion is to be followed by a personal spiritual "walk," which is to be characterized by growth in holiness.[24]

This onward growth in holiness is described by James Houston as: "the outworking of the grace of God in the soul of the man, beginning with conversion to conclusion in death or Christ's Second Advent. It is marked by growth and maturity in a Christ-like life."[25] Evangelicals believe that salvation and faith is a matter of personal experience rather than communal. Piety among them is largely individualistic. *Bible reading* means private Bible reading, *prayer* means private prayer, *salvation* means being saved as an

---

[24] Grenz, 47.

[25] James M. Houston, 'Spirituality' in *Evangelical Dictionary of Theology*, Walter A. Elwell, eds.(Grand Rapids, Michigan: Baker Publishing Group, 2001), 1047.

individual, *being in Christ* means having a personal relationship with Jesus, *the empowerment of the Holy Spirit* means being capable as an individual to act or follow the direction of the Holy Spirit.[26] In this case, therefore, salvation can neither be inherited nor conferred. In the decision for or against Christ and in the receipt of reward and judgment on the Last Day, each believer stands alone.

Because spirituality is essentially an individual matter, it requires personal diligence and applications of one's resources. Evangelicals continually admonish each other to take charge of their lives and apply themselves to the task of spiritual growth. As a result, strong emphasis is placed on discipleship and spiritual discipline which include, but are not limited to, daily reading of the Word of God and prayer–*quiet time,* living a life of obedience to Christ, love, holiness, humility, simplicity, philanthropism, fellowshipping with others and living a life of integrity on a daily basis.[27]

The direct and personal fellowship with God is not mediated directly by church, liturgy or sacrament. This helps explain why evangelical spirituality has not developed a universal system of spiritual disciplines in the way Catholicism has. For evangelical spirituality, the system is more fluid because of its focus on personal faith relationship with God and on his glory rather than the disciplines per se, or even believers and their spiritual development. It is open for every practitioner and spiritual guide to develop the basic principles in a way that seems appropriate to their own needs and context.[28]

---

[26] Grenz, *Revisioning Evangelical Theology,* 50.

[27] Ibid., 51.

[28] Nathan Finn, 'On Evangelical Spirituality' in http://www.nathanfinn.com/2013/03/28/on-evangelical-spirituality/ Posted on March 28, 2013. See also David Parker, 'Evangelical Spirituality Reviewed,' *Evangelical Quarterly* 63:2 (1991), 129-31.

The individualistic nature of evangelical spirituality does not neglect the importance of fellowship and accountability to brethren in the community of faith that we belong. Consequently, we continually check up on others and on ourselves. "Are you growing in the Lord? Are you walking with God? Are you developing a friendship with the Lord? Do you find that your life is being changed? Such questions become statements of mutual caring once a person has joined the fold. As an expression of this ethos, we heartily sing: *What a friend we have in Jesus!*"[29]

Thus, in evangelical spirituality, the Christian life is one of pilgrimage, with the believer walking humbly as an alien in this world, answering to the Lord from heaven and looking towards the final hope, which is the consummation of all in God's Eternal Kingdom. This spirituality is *world denying* in the sense that it does not credit this life and this world with ultimate autonomy. However, it is also *world affirming* in that it confesses that this world is God's creation and therefore not to be abused or ignored but to be used carefully and sensitively for his glory. It also affirms that this world is the medium and context of salvation and Christian service and is ultimately to be redeemed.[30]

The fourth *essential* nature of evangelicalism is evangelism. The name of the movement, *Evangelicals,* was derived from the Greek noun εὐαγγέλιον, meaning good news. Evangelical Christians are strongly motivated to share the Gospel either one-to-one, by campaigns or through organised missions employing diverse platforms and opportunities. Emphasis is placed on the Great Commission's call to share with the world the Christian message of salvation through

---

[29] Grenz, 47.
[30] Nathan Finn, 'On Evangelical Spirituality' in http://www.nathanfinn.com/2013/03/28/on-evangelical-spirituality/ Posted on March 28, 2013.

Christ, and to be publicly baptized as a confession of faith.[31] This is central to the identity and ethos of evangelicals around the world. So, to be an evangelical is to be unconditionally involved in evangelism and missions. There are other central issues such as: Assurance of Salvation, the Second Advent of Christ, Rapture of the Saints, Priesthood of all believers, the discipline of prayer and fasting, love, forgiveness, humility and generosity, to highlight just a few; space will not allow us to examine this in detail in this particular study.

Religion versus Spirituality: A Biblical Perspective

On the surface, one would think that religion and spirituality are synonymous and that there should be no difference in their definitions. But that is certainly not the case. While religion and spirituality are interdependent, their meanings are different in that the two exist to serve different ends. The terms are related, and yet, distinct when it comes to matters of faith. Religion denotes 'a set of beliefs concerning the cause, nature and purpose of the universe, usually involving devotional and ritual observances and a moral code.'[32] In contrast, *spirituality* can be defined as 'the quality of being spiritual.'[33] The table below is drawn based on the *Compelling Truth's* description of the differences between religion and spirituality[34]:

---

[31] Traci Schumacher, '5 Beliefs that Sets Evangelical Apart from other Christians' in https://www.newsmax.com/fastfeatures/evangelical-christians-beliefs/2015/04/02/id/636050/ Posted April 2, 2015.

[32] 'Is there a Difference between Religion and Spirituality' in *Compelling Truth*: https://www.compellingtruth.org/difference-religion-spirituality.html/ Accessed on April 11, 2020.

[33] Ibid.

[34] Ibid.

Religion	Spirituality
Religion's focus is the content of one's belief and the outworking of that belief.	Spirituality focuses on the process of becoming more attuned to unworldly affairs.
A religious person accepts a certain set of beliefs as true and observes a certain set of rituals.	In contrast, spirituality is the fact of being spiritual and is usually evidenced by the act of doing spiritual things.
Religion usually promotes a creed and has a defined code of ethics; it is tangible.	Spirituality is more abstract than religion. Spirituality exists in the nebulous realm of the undefinable.

The definitions above, according to Compelling *Truth* indicate that 'the major difference between religion and spirituality is one of believing and being. While religion focuses more on the content of one's belief and the outworking of the same, spirituality focuses on the process of fleshing out or becoming more inwardly attuned to one's belief.'[35] Religion focuses more on general tenets of a given faith while spirituality is concerned with individual belief and practicing of the faith. So, by implication, it is possible to be religious without being spiritual. Following this understanding, Christianity as a religion could be defined as the faith based on the person and teachings of Jesus. Spirituality means believing in Jesus Christ and the holistic practice of his teachings.

It is important to note that there are different types of spirituality. Unlike other religions, there is no dichotomy between Christianity and spirituality. 'Biblically speaking, religion and spirituality should be united, and the end result should be good works to the glory of

---

[35] Ibid.

God.'³⁶ Four scriptures are instructive in putting the biblical position on Christianity and spirituality into perspective: Matthew 5:16, James 1:27, 2 Timothy 3:5 and Romans 12:1-2. These scriptures suggest a deep connection between the 'content of one's belief' and 'process of being inwardly attuned to one's belief.' Additionally, these scriptures opine that a Christian is not truly a Christian until having had a salvation encounter with Jesus Christ and becoming committed to a lifelong walk with and work for Jesus. In this book, Evangelical Spirituality is viewed as Christianity expressed, based on the Evangelical ethos and practices, with specific focus on the transformation of individual Christians.

Evangelical Christianity in the Contemporary African Context

According to Stanley Grenz, "Spirituality is the quest, under the direction of the Holy Spirit but with the cooperation of the believer, for holiness. It is the pursuit of the life lived to the glory of God, in union with Christ and out of obedience to the Holy Spirit."³⁷ The New Testament sets forth two broad directions of aspiration within the context of the spiritual pilgrimage. The document articulates both a call for a holy detachment from the world and an admonition for dedicated involvement in the world. On one hand, Christians are challenged to walk the narrow road to the Kingdom.

Consequently, spirituality is inward and quietistic. It consists of the denial of self, a mystical union with Christ and an ascetic approach to life, nurtured by the heavenly vision. On the other hand, believers are admonished to live in the world and serve others. Spirituality is outward and active. It requires compassion, mercy and a zealous

---

[36] Ibid.
[37] Grenz, 42.

desire for justice, guided by a vision of what the world could be like.[38] Unfortunately, these features are no more visible among many evangelicals in Africa today. The prevailing outcome of our impact on the African society is enough reason to substantiate my submission.

The Church in Africa is fast losing its moral credibility. The Church no longer possesses the respect it used to have few decades back. Many *Church leaders* and *Christians* are seen to be involved in different kinds of fraudulent practices to which unbelievers are known. There is much corruption in the church as there is outside. Church leaders who remain vanguards of truth are like lone voices in the wilderness. Yet, the Church is expected to be the conscience of society by challenging the social menaces of injustice, poor leadership, bad governance, corruption, impunity, poverty and unemployment, increasing armed robbery, banditry, kidnapping, drug addiction, substance abuse, examination malpractice, bribery, communal clashes and religious unrest prevalent in our continent. This is presenting the Gospel of Jesus with humanity in mind.

But can these battles be fought by a Church that is itself corrupt and whose emphasis is on *things* rather than living the life of Christ and being the light of God to the world? Disappointedly, even within the church, the scourges of commercialization, self-enrichment, materialism, unexplained mushrooming of churches, *false prophets*, dodgy pastors, false doctrines, lack of discipleship and unchristian practices are some of the factors crippling the moral greatness of the church in this part of the world today. While this development is not peculiar to Africa, the volume of this disturbing music seems to be louder here than elsewhere. So, the Evangelical Movement has a great and urgent role to play in confronting these issues to the glory of God and to the profit of his Kingdom.

---

[38] Grenz, *Revisioning Evangelical Theology,* 42.

CHAPTER FOUR

PENTECOSTAL AND EVANGELICAL CHRISTIANITY IN AFRICA: SOULMATES OR STRANGE BEDFELLOWS?

Pentecostalism occupies a central place in the study of contemporary world Christianity. Its growth and expansion in the last half-century have been unprecedented and phenomenal. This brand of Christianity has become a representative brand of Christianity on the African continent and globally. Besides the Roman Catholic Church, no other brand of Christianity in Africa can boast of similar numeric explosion like the Pentecostal movements. Following this development, it would be inappropriate to study Evangelicalism on the continent without situating and underscoring its relationship with Pentecostal-Charismatic Christianity.

Relationship between Pentecostal and Evangelical Christianity

There is a sustained relational tension in Africa about what constitutes Evangelical denominations. While this challenge is not peculiar to Africa, the diversity in practices and classifications are more pronounced in Africa than elsewhere. This challenge is more from historic missionary denominations who are direct offshoots of protestant Christianity. These are historic missionary denominations that have links with the Great Britain Evangelicalism of the 1700s. In Africa, there exists a notion that there are differences between Evangelical denominations and their Pentecostal-Charismatic counterparts. These differences are largely based on theological, doctrinal, liturgical, and ethical issues, as well as their traditions and genealogies.

One of the most visible areas of difficulty in the convergence of evangelical and Pentecostal-Charismatic Christianity is *glossolalia*. At this point, it is essential that we review again the central ethos of Evangelicalism: compare and contrast to that of Pentecostalism. This will help us isolate the (common) areas of agreements and disagreements in both movements. Evangelical Christians believe, first, that Jesus Christ is the Son of God. Second, they believe that there is need for personal salvation in Christ. Third is the belief that the Bible is the Word of God and has the final authority on the whole of life. And finally, they believe in evangelistic and activistic living and involvement. Pentecostals also believe in all the positions cited above–but with an additional position in *glossolalia*. Pentecostals hold that being born-again must be accompanied with the evidence of speaking in tongues. In the words of Amos Yong, 'Pentecostals hold that speaking in tongues is a signal or evidence of baptism in the Holy Spirit.'[1] This is the most pronounced difference between the Evangelicals and Pentecostals.

The Pentecostal emphasis on speaking in tongues and overt expression of grace gifts (*charisma*) best underscores the theological, doctrinal, liturgical and hermeneutical departures of Evangelical and Pentecostal. These differences are also obvious in modes of worship. Some mainline historic denominations do believe in speaking in tongues but hold an exception to the Pentecostal approach to speaking in tongues and expression of grace gifts in public. But is the issue of speaking in tongues big enough to knockout other areas of commonalities between the historic Evangelical and Pentecostal denominations? What happens to the historical bond that the movements share? Some scholars have viewed Pentecostalism as a part of Evangelicalism. Reflecting on the relationship between Evangelical and Pentecostal traditions, Amos Yong explains that:

> Some insist that Pentecostalism is a subset of evangelicalism - especially those who understand the evangelical tradition's genealogy as stretching back to the Reformation churches of the sixteenth century, including those who identify John Wesley as the "grandfather" of Pentecostalism (through the Holiness movement of the nineteenth century), or who view continental pietism and even Puritan revivalism as contributing to the Pentecostal DNA. Others say that in a more technical sense Pentecostal origins in the early twentieth century–whether at Azusa Street or at Topeka, Kansas, disputed among

---

[1] Amos Yong, 'Evangelical, Pentecostals and Charismatics: A Difficult Relationship or Promising Convergence?' in *Fuller Studio*: *https://fullerstudio.fuller.edu/evangelicals-pentecostals-and-charismatics/* Accessed on April 9, 2020.

historians–preceded that of the formal organization of modern (at least American) evangelicalism, particularly as initiated by the founding of the National Association of Evangelicals in 1942.[2]

Based on this explanation by Yong, we can submit that the earliest form of Pentecostal movements, especially its holiness taxonomy, has a strong connection with revival and evangelistic efforts of John Wesley. This historical link suggests that Pentecostal in its earliest form is a continuation of the Evangelical movement. But this is not to deny the fact that the Azusa Street revival remains the most prominent of all of the origins of global Pentecostal movements in the modern world.

So, 'whether Pentecostal believers are also or always evangelicals depends on how either is defined.'[3] According to Yong, 'political, democratic, economic, cultural realities of our local and global context may colour how Pentecostals and Evangelicals are defined and understood.'[4] The following questions raised by Yong on the subject are apt for conclusion on this subject:

> Would some Pentecostals wish also to be accepted as evangelicals because of the respectability that comes with such designation and in order to escape the opprobrium that still might tar the Pentecostal label? On the other hand, might some evangelicals think that the pentecostalizing and charismatizing nature of global Christianity renders the Pentecostal label more advantageous in at least certain contexts?

---

[2] Ibid.
[3] Ibid.
[4] Ibid.

And none of the preceding engages the central theological and doctrinal issues in the balance.

Based on the background above, this study holds that Pentecostalism is a subset of Evangelical Christianity. Rather than being exclusive, this book adopts an inclusive, open and generous definition of Evangelical Christianity which converges both movements under one broad categorization, Evangelicalism. Having established the relationship between Evangelical Christianity and Pentecostal Christianity, it is important now that we illuminate the relationship between Pentecostal and Charismatic Christianity.

Pentecostal and Charismatic Movements: Any Difference?

The terms Pentecostalism and Charismatic movements have been used interchangeably in scholarship over the years.[5] It is therefore important to define these terms based on the cardinal and general ethos of what makes a movement Pentecostal or Charismatic. The definition given to Pentecostal movements by Kwabena Asamoah-Gyadu best describes the usage of the term in this study. According to Kwabena:

> Pentecostalism can be understood as that stream of Christianity that emphasizes personal salvation in Christ as a transformative experience wrought by the Holy Spirit; and in which such pneumatic phenomenon as speaking in tongues, prophecies,

---

[5] See Allan Anderson, *An Introduction to Pentecostalism* (Cambridge: Cambridge University Press, 2004), 13; and Ogbu Kalu, *African Pentecostalism*, 9.

visions, healing, miracles, and signs and wonders in general, are sought, accepted, valued, and consciously encouraged among members as evidence of the active presence of God's Spirit.[6]

The experiences defined in the quote above are tied to the biblical principles defined in Acts 2:28 and John 3:5. This study follows the conventional usage and retain *Pentecostals* for Christian denominations claiming the Biblical Pentecostal heritage as found in the Gospel of St. John and Acts of the Apostles cited above.

However, 'the differences in Pentecostal/Charismatic phenomena make the issue of definitions and nomenclature important for[7] any study in Pentecostalism. The term *Charisma* comes from a Greek phrase αρισματα πνευματικα which is derived from Paul's expression, *Gift of the Spirit* (1Corinthians 12-14), and which he uses to refer to those 'extraordinary graces' attributable to the experience of the Holy Spirit.'[8] Millard Erickson goes further when he elaborates that *Charisma* could sometimes be 'referred to as remarkable gifts, miraculous gifts, special gifts, sign gifts, or charismatic gifts. The last being a somewhat redundant expression, since Καρισμα (charisma) basically means gifts.'[9] But over time, the term has, according to Erickson, been frequently associated with faith healing, exorcism of demons and especially *glossolalia*

---

[6] Kwabena Asamaoh-Gyadu, *'Born of Water and Spirit': Pentecostal/Charismatic Christianity in Africa,* Ogbu, U. Kalu, ed., in *African Christianity: An African Story,* Series 5 Vol. 3 (Pretoria: Print Center, 2005), 398.

[7] Ibid., 398.

[8] Ibid.

[9] Millard J. Erickson, 'The Miraculous Gifts Today', In *Introduction Christian Doctrine* (Grand Rapids: Baker Academic, 2001), 281. See also Wayne Grudem, *Systematic Theology* (Nottingham: Inter-Varsity Press, 1994), 1237.

(γλωσσωλαλια) or speaking in tongues.[10] Thus, *glossolalia* is one of the issues that stresses the difference between Pentecostal and Charismatic movements.

Beyond *glossolalia*, Grudem defines the Charismatic Movement as 'a term referring to any group or people that trace their historical origin to the charismatic renewal movement of the 1960s and 1970s.'[11] He stresses further that, 'those groups seek to practice all the spiritual gifts mentioned in the New Testament but, unlike many Pentecostal denominations, allow differing viewpoint on whether baptism of the Holy Spirit is subsequent to conversion and whether tongues is a sign of baptism in the Holy Spirit.'[12] These groups seek the restoration of the Church by employing the spectacular gifts of the Holy Spirit given to every believer in the church.[13] The Charismatic movement refers to all manifestations of Pentecostal-like Christianity that is in some ways different from classical Pentecostalism in affiliation or in doctrine.[14] While Pentecostalism has denominational configurations, Charismatic Christianity is largely expressed within historic churches. In this book, the expression *Charismatic* is restricted to Pentecostal renewal movements that operate within historic mission denominations[15] or any such parachurch organisations.

---

[10] Ibid., 281.

[11] Wayne Grudem, *Systematic Theology* (Nottingham: Inter-Varsity Press, 1994), 1237.

[12] Grudem, 1237-8.

[13] J.D. Douglas and Earle E Cairns, eds. 'Charismata' In *The New International Dictionary of the Christian Church* (Grand Rapids: Zondervan Publishing House, 1978), 211-2.

[14] Stanly M Burgess and Edwuard M Van Der Maas, eds. 'Charismatic Movement' In *The New International Dictionary of Pentecostal and Charismatic Movements* (Grand Rapids: Zondervan, 2003), 477.

[15] Asamoah-Gyadu, *'Born of Water and Spirit'*, 389.

Nigerian Pentecostalism within the African Christian Tapestry

Pentecostalism is the fastest growing stream of Christianity in the world today.[16] Its growth has been rapid and phenomenal. Scholars have attributed the unprecedented growth of Pentecostalism to a number of factors.[17] Peterson Douglas, while citing the Latin America experience, agrees with the aforementioned submission. According to Douglas, 'in less than a century, the Pentecostal movement evolved from a small rag-tag band of Christian believers to a worldwide movement with an estimated 500 million adherents.'[18] It would not be an overstatement to mention at this juncture that Africa is one of the few places that Pentecostalism has witnessed unprecedented growth in recent times.

In the words of Harvey Cox, "the rise, growth and impact of Pentecostalism are some of the most significant developments in African Christianity since the middle of the twentieth century."[19] This points to the impacts of Pentecostalism on Africans as well as to their societies. In Africa, it is difficult to divorce people's religious lives from their culture, and indeed, life itself. According to Gerald McDermott, this observation is not only peculiar to Africans but has its foundation in the Word of God. Gerald argues that religions are living and breathing beings that have souls integrated to the life

---

[16] Ibid., 387-409.

[17] Mark Shaw, *Global Awakening: How 21st Century Revivals Triggered a Christian Revolution* (Downers Grove: IVP Academic, 2010). 11.

[18] Peterson Douglas, 'Latin *America Pentecostalism: Social Capital, Networks, and Politics*' (PNEUMA: *The Journal of the Society for Pentecostal Studies*: Volume 26, No 2, Fall 2004). 293-306.

[19] Douglas, 293.

of the society which they belong.[20] Religion is an integral part of the African people, and it has impact on their societies.

Pentecostalism as a brand of Christianity has not only contributed to the development of Sub-Saharan African societies but also serves as a challenge to other brands of Christianity on the continent. Within various regions of the world, the Pentecostal Movement has grown to the point where t it now challenges the temper of Christian practices, doctrinal bastions, revered polities, liturgies and muted or liberalized dimensions of Christian ethics.[21] It must be mentioned that the astonishing growth of Pentecostalism in Africa should be understood within a larger perspective that all religious forms are growing. The Roman Catholic Church remains the largest Christian body in most of Africa.[22] The most astonishing demographical survey of world Christianity involve Pentecostals and Charismatic Christians. For instance, "There were 981,000 of these souls in 1900; there are more than 643, 661,000 today; and there are projected to be over one billion Charismatics and Pentecostals in 2050."[23] According to George Weigel, the most extraordinary Christian growth over the past century has come in Africa: home to 8.7 million Christians in 1900, 542 million today, and perhaps 1.2 billion by 2050, when there will be as many African Christians as

---

[20] Gerald, R. McDermott, *God's Rivals: Insights from Biblical and Early Church* (Downer Groves: Inter-Varsity Press, 2007), 11.

[21] Kalu Ogbu, *African Pentecostalism: An Introduction* (New oxford: Oxford University Press, 2008), 11.

[22] George Weigel, 'World Christianity by the Numbers' in *First Thing*:https:// www.firstthings.com/web-exclusives/2015/02/world-christianity-by-the-numbers,Posted 25th February, 2015, Accessed on 28th September, 2016.

[23] George Weigel, 'World Christianity by the Numbers.' See also 'Christian Movements and Denominations' in *Pew Research Center Religion and Public Life*:http://www.pewforum.org/2011/12/19/global-christianity-movements-and-denominations/ Posted on 19th December, 2011; Accessed on 28th September, 2016.

Latin American and European Christians combined.[24] The concerns of scholars have been more on the shortness of the period within which Pentecostalism grew to such a numeric phenomenal.

Describing the Ghanaian context, Ogbu Kalu explains that, "Nobody in Ghana is unaware of the shift. Everyone is aware of [their] Charismatic prayer centers, their all-night services, their churches, conventions, and Bible Schools, their new buildings (or the schools, cinemas and halls they rent), their bumper stickers and banners, and particularly the posters that everywhere advertise an enormous range of forthcoming activities. Everyone is aware of the media efforts. Above all everyone knows of the new religious superstars.'[25] While the historic churches remain steady, there was a general awareness of a new wave of Pentecostalism-Charismatic influence on the church in a short span of twenty years (1979-2000) of its great move in Ghana.[26] Kalu's explanation points to the influence Pentecostalism had on other historic churches in Ghana within just a short period of time.

When discussing the phenomenal growth of Pentecostal Christianity in Africa, Nigeria occupies a strategic position in the dialogue. Scholars have long observed that Nigeria is experiencing the fastest growth of Christianity in Africa, with Pentecostal churches making a significant contribution to the development.[27] Brian Stanley,

---

[24] George Weigel, 'World Christianity by the Numbers.'

[25] Kalu Ogbu, *African Pentecostalism: An Introduction*, 6.

[26] Ibid.

[27] Asamoah-Gyadu Kwabena, 'Pentecostal Media Images and Religious globalization in Sub-Saharan Africa,' in P. Horsfield, M.E. Hess and A. Medrano (Eds.), *Belief in Media: Cultural Perspectives on Media and Christianity, Media Development*, No. 2, 2004, 17-22. See also Dayo Fakoya, 'Gospel of Materialism-Nigerian Pentecostalism and Hypocrisy, *Tribune*, 28th August, 2008, Lagos, 16. Godwin Okon, 'Televangelism and Socio-Political Mobilization of Pentecostal in Port-Harcourt Metropolis: A KAP Survey,' in *Religion, Media and Politics in Africa*, No. 1 (Vol. V), 2011, 64-5. Jenkins, *The Next Christendom*, 173.

in recent work, describes Nigeria as the 'epicenter of the Pentecostal movement in the English speaking world.'[28] Acknowledging this development, Asamoah-Gyadu corroborates that, 'Nigeria is Africa's most populous nation and the location of one of the most vibrant Christian communities in World Christianity.'[29] Nigeria, as the most populous country in Africa, could have contributed to the position that Pentecostal movements occupy on the continent.

Nigeria is a deeply religious country.[30] It is a nation of a population of between 150 and 170 million people, and 250 ethnic groups.[31] When speaking of the significant Christian population as one of the factors in favor of the influence of Nigerian Pentecostalism on the continent of Africa, we should also mention the huge presence of Islam in the country. The estimates of the number of Christians and Muslim in Nigeria vary. The country's inhabitants are roughly divided between Christians, who live predominantly in the south and central parts, and Muslims, a great majority of whom live in the north and southwest. About 10% of the population, especially Igbo and Yoruba people, practice traditional indigenous religion.[32] If these figures are anything to go by, then the Christian population in Nigeria is immense when you compare it to their counterparts in other African countries.

---

[28] Brian Stanley, *The Global Diffusion of Evangelicalism* (Nottingham: Inter-Varsity Press, 2013), 202.

[29] Asamoah-Gyadu Kwabena, 'Pentecostal Media Images and Religious globalization in Sub-Saharan Africa', 17-22.

[30] Caroline Varin, *Boko Haram and the War on Terror* (Santa Barbara: ABC-CLIO, 2016), 7. See also Toyin Falola, and Bukola Adeyemi Oyeniyi, *Nigeria: Africa in Focus* (Santa Barbara: ABC-CLIO, 2015), xv.

[31] Caroline Varin, *Boko Haram and the War on Terror*, 11.

[32] Toyin Falola, and Bukola Adeyemi Oyeniyi, *Nigeria: Africa in Focus* (Santa Barbara: ABC-CLIO, 2015), xv.

Nigeria's population constitutes half of Africa's people.[33] This makes Nigeria the most populated nation in Africa. In the words of Peter Wagner and Joseph Thompson, 'one of every five black persons in the world lives in Nigeria.'[34] For instance, out of the over 70 million members of the Anglican Communion worldwide, Nigeria alone claims about 20 million baptized Anglicans.[35] In his recent study 'Releasing the Trigger: The Nigerian factor in Global Christianity', Allan Effa corroborates Wagner and Thompson's perspectives when he submits that, 'The strength of mainline Nigerian Christianity has been most evident in the Anglican Communion. It is fair to say that the very heart of the Anglican community has been transplanted to Africa. The Church of Nigeria alone, numbering about 19 million, accounts for 25% of all Anglicans in the world.'[36] This is a clear indication of the population impact of the Nigerian Church in Africa and on World Christianity today. That is probably why Nigeria has been regarded as 'a giant of today's Christian landscape'.[37] Of the six continents of the world, Africa is currently experiencing the most accelerated rate of church growth at 2.62% per year. Asia (including China) is second with 2.12%, while as a point of contrast, North America is only seeing 0.81% per annual growth.[38]

---

[33] Falola and Oyeniyi, xv. See also Peter Wagner and Joseph Thompson, *Out of Africa: How the Spiritual Explosion Among Nigerians Is Impacting the World* (Ventura: Regal Books, 2004), 8.

[34] Wagner and Thompson, 8.

[35] Jenkins, 59.

[36] Allan F Effa, 'Releasing the Trigger: The Nigerian Factor in Global Christianity' in *International Bulletin of Missionary Research*, Vol. 37, No. 4 (October 2013), 216.

[37] Wagner and Thompson, 8.

[38] George Weigel, "World Christianity by the Numbers" in *First Thing*:https://www.firstthings.com/web-exclusives/2015/02/world-christianity-by-the-numbers,Posted 25th February, 2015, Accessed on 28th September, 2016. See also Wagner and Thompson, 8.

Nigerian Pentecostalism has been described as one of the most explosive brands of Christianity in the world today. This brand of Christianity has spread like fire and has proliferated outside the shores of Nigeria to various parts of the world. According to Kamate, 'Nigerian Pentecostals have . . . exerted significant influence upon Pentecostals in other regions of Africa, thus lending credence to the claim that some of the largest congregations across Africa have been planted by Nigerian denominations."[39]

In *The Next Christendom,* Philip Jenkins argues that no serious research can be done on the current explosion of the Pentecostal-Charismatic movement in modern World Christianity without mention of Nigerian Pentecostalism.[40] The growth of this brand of Christianity has attracted and keeps attracting scholarly investigation from different fields of human inquiry.[41]

As earlier discussed, the issues that Pentecostalism is addressing clearly indicate why it has been able to attract large numbers of people in the last couple of years. The growth factor is one of the reasons Pentecostalism is the fastest growing stream of Christianity in the world in recent time.[42] The same factor, meeting the needs of the

---

[39] Kamate Rigobert, 'Pentecostalism in Kinshasa: Maintaining Multiple Church Membership, Tanzania,' in *African Communication Research,* Vol. 2, No. 1, 2009, 149. See also Godwin Okon, 'Televangelism and Socio-Political Mobilization of Pentecostal in Port-Harcourt Metropolis: A KAP Survey,' in *Religion, Media and Politics in Africa,* No. 1 (Vol. V), 2011, 65.

[40] Philip Jenkins, *The Next Christendom: The Coming of Global Christianity* (Oxford: Oxford University Press, 2002).

[41] Nimi Waribiko, *Nigerian Pentecostalism* (Rochester, NY: University of Rochester Press, 2014), 2

[42] Kwabena J. Asamoah-Gyadu, 'Born of Water and Spirit: Pentecostal/Charismatic Christianity' in *African Christianity: An African Story,* Kalu, U. Ogbu, ed. Series 5 Vol. 3 (Pretoria: Print Center, 2005), 387-409.

people-mostly the poor-[43] is traceable to the growth of Pentecostal Churches Nigeria. It is not uncommon to find Pentecostal Churches, like Winner's Chapel, having an over 50,000 seat auditorium – the world's largest-[44] and Redeemed Christian Church of God's Holy Ghost Congress attracting millions of people during a one week programme held annually in Nigeria.[45] Pentecostal Churches with massive attendance are very common in Nigeria, and that is the reason Nigeria is always important to the study of contemporary World Christianity.

Peter Wagner, after several visits to a number of Pentecostal assemblies and meetings in Nigeria, noted that, 'Nigeria is a giant of today's Christian landscape. I say "a" giant rather than "the" giant because Mainland China may rival Nigeria as the epicenter of Christian power in the world today. Having said that, of all the countries to which we have free access, I would place Nigeria atop the list of those with a dynamic explosion of the Christian faith in our times.'[46] Wagner adds further that, 'Nigeria can be considered as the center of gravity as far as the dramatic, visible, and outward manifestation of the presence of the kingdom of God is concerned.'[47]

---

[43] Alan Isaacson, *Deeper Life: The Extraordinary Growth of the Deeper Life Bible Church* (London: Hodder and Stoughton, 1990), 19.

[44] Albert Babajide Adeboye, 'Effects of Industrial Revolution on Ecclesiastical Architecture in Nigeria: The Case of Faith Tabernacle at Ota' in *International Journal of Management, Information Technology and Engineering*, Vol. 3, Issue 2 (Feb., 2015), 28, 34.

[45] Asonzeh Ukah, 'Building God's City: The Political Economy of Prayer Camps in Nigeria' in *International Journal of Urban and Regional Research* (Sept., 2016), Access on www.wiley.com/doi/10.1111/1468-2427/full, 1. See also Wagner and Thompson, 166-167.

[46] C. Peter Wagner and Joseph Thompson, *Out of Africa: How the Spiritual Explosion among Nigerian is Impacting the World* (California: Regal Books, 2004), 10-11.

[47] Ibid.

Pentecostal Christianity has continued to grow in an unprecedented manner in Nigeria.

In a similar observation, observers of African Christianity have noted that Nigeria is not only Africa's most populous nation but also the location of one of the most vibrant Christian communities in World Christianity. Since the 1970s, Nigeria's religious landscape has been transformed by the emergence of new, locally instituted Pentecostal churches, with a more modern and global orientation.[48]

Nigerian Pentecostals have also exerted significant influences upon Pentecostals in other regions of Africa and further afield through transnational exchanges of ministry, media and theological education. Nigerian pastors are regularly invited to speak at conferences in such countries as Ghana, Kenya, Uganda, Zambia and South Africa, and some of the largest congregations across Africa have been planted by Nigerian denominations."[49] Many of the ingredients that make up the religious repertoire of Nigerian Pentecostal churches are found within African Pentecostalism generally. Burgess adds that, 'due to rapid expansion and adept use of media technologies, these churches have attracted the attention of scholars from a variety of disciplines.'[50] Anderson, speaking of

---

[48] Benjamin C.D. Diara, and Nkechinyere G. Onah, 'The Phenomenal Growth of Pentecostalism in the Contemporary Nigerian Society: A Challenge to Mainline Churches' in *Mediterranean Journal of Social Sciences,* Vol. 5, No. 6 (April, 2014), 395-6.

[49] For example, the largest churches in Kenya, Tanzania, Ghana, and Zimbabwe were started by Nigerians. In 2001, the Accra congregation of the Nigerian-initiated Winners' Chapel was attracting around 13,000 to its Sunday worship meeting, and its pastor was a Ghanaian (See Richard Burgess, 'Nigerian Pentecostal Theology in Global Perspective' *PentecoStudies,* Vol. 7, no.2, 2008, (29-63), 31; and Paul Gifford, *Ghana's New Christianity,* London: Hurst and Company, 2004, 56).

[50] Burgess, 31.

Nigeria, says, "West Africa is one of the most discussed regions of the world as far as Pentecostalism is concerned, having rapidly become one of the most prominent and influential religious movements across this region."[51] This is evidence scholars have given to acknowledge the growth of Nigerian Pentecostalism.

Nigerian Pentecostalism and Its Appropriation of Media

Before the outbreak of COVID-19, African Pentecostalism was ahead of other brands of Christianity in its appropriation of media. Recent developments in Nigerian Christianity and its film industry have attracted robust and ongoing scholarly interest. Scholars have attributed the exponential growth of African Pentecostalism partly to its appropriation of media.[52] No other brand of African Christianity has utilized media more than the Pentecostal movements.[53] The tremendous expansion of the Nigerian Christian film industry is one typical example of how African Christianity is making use of the

---

[51] Allan Anderson, *An Introduction to African Pentecostalism* (Cambridge: Cambridge University Press, 2004), 115.

[52] J. Kwabena Asamoah-Gyadu, 'Pentecostalism Media Images and Religious Globalization in Sub-Saharan Africa,' in *Belief in Media: Cultural Perspectives in Media and Christianity,* Peter Horsfield, Mary E. Hess, et. al., eds., (Hants, Ashgate, 2004), 65-67. See also Afe Adogame, 'Online for God: Media Negotiation and African Religious Movements,' in *Who is Afraid of the Holy Ghost*, Afe Adogame, ed., (Trenton, NJ: Africa World Press, 2011), 223-235.

[53] Philomena Njeri Mwaura, 'Gendered Appropriation of Mass Media in Kenyan Christianities: A Comparison of Two Women-Led African Instituted Churches in Kenya,' in *Interpreting Contemporary Christianity: Global Processes and Local Identities,*OgbuU. Kalu, and Alaine Low, eds., (Grand Rapids: William B. Eerdmans Publishing Company, 2008), 274-295.

media to further its cause.⁵⁴ A big part of the Nigerian Christian film industry is dominated by producers within the Pentecostal religion.⁵⁵ According to Asamoah-Gyadu, 'Pentecostal appropriation of media, of recent not only serves as its identity but an important means of spreading its agenda and the pentecostalization of Christianity and societies in Africa.'⁵⁶ Despite these exploits, it is essential to note that Pentecostals have been criticized for promoting enchanted Christianity, power, apolitical contents and the commercialization of the gospel through the media products. These have been observed as some of the factors reducing the impact of the Christian message in the African public space.

In his study of Nigerian Pentecostalism and its appropriation of media, Asonzeh F. K. Ukah argues that Christian media are calculated attempts by Pentecostal institutions to make money from their audiences.⁵⁷ Ukah contends that the images of Pentecostal pastors portrayed in Nigerian Pentecostal films are aimed at changing the tastes of film consumers. These film producers make use of their understanding of the Nigerian social and religious context in films to capture the imaginations of their film consumers.⁵⁸ The

---

⁵⁴ J. Kwabena Asamoah-Gyadu, 'Mediating Spiritual Power: African Christianity, Transnationalism and the Media,' in *Religion Crossing Boundaries*, Afe Adogame and James V. Spickard, eds., (Boston: Brill, 2010), 87-103.

⁵⁵ Ibid. See also Ruth Marshall-Fratani, 'Mediating the Global and the Local in Nigerian Pentecostalism,' *Journal of Religion in Africa*, Vol. 28, No. 3 (1998), 278-315.

⁵⁶ J. Kwabena Asamoah-Gyadu, *Contemporary Pentecostal Christianity: Interpretations from an African Context* (Oxford: Regnum Books International, 2013), xiii.

⁵⁷ Asonzeh Ukah, *A New Paradigm of Pentecostal Power: A Study of the Redeemed Christian Church of God in Nigeria* (Trenton, NJ: Africa World Press, Inc., 2008), 145-152.

⁵⁸ Asonzeh F. K. Ukah, 'Advertising God: Nigerian Christian Video-Films and the Power of Consumer Culture,' *Journal of Religion in Africa*, Vol. 33, No. 2, Religion and the Media (May. 2003), 203-231. See also Asonzeh Ukah, 'Banishing Miracles: Politics and Policies of Religious Broadcasting in Nigeria,' *Journal of Politics and Religion in Africa*, Vol. 1, No. 5, Religion, Media and Politics in Africa (2011), 39-59.

notion of commercialization of media texts portrays the church as a marketplace. While Ukah's focus is not particularly on the representations of Pentecostal pastors, his reference to Pentecostal appropriation of indigenous culture in their media products takes us in a new direction in the discourse. Asonzeh situates Nigerian Pentecostal practices, the representation of its pastors and its appropriation of media within the African cultural milieu. Ukah describes Pentecostal pastors not just as people with strong financial means, but as men and women who occupy important places within the Nigerian religious and cultural milieu. This experience is tantamount to what Walter Ihejirika, Professor of Anthropology and Communication theory at the University of Port Harcourt, Nigeria, refers to as the convergence theory. In his comparative study of the Roman Catholic Church of Nigeria and the Nigerian Pentecostal-Charismatic movement, Ihejirika argues that the phenomenal growth of Pentecostal Christianity in Africa is due to its appropriation of the convergence theory. The theory, according to him, is the equivalent translation of indigenous African worldviews into Christianity.[59] Ihejirika argues:

> I would propose that a convergence theory offers the best framework to explain the religious phenomenon in Africa. That is, the best explanation of what kind of religious practices and use of the media are emerging in terms of the areas of congruence or convergence between traditional

---

[59] Walter Ihejirika C., 'Research on Media, Religion and Culture in Africa: Current Trends and Dialogue,' *African Journal of Communication Research*, Vol. 2, No. 1 (2009), 1-60. See also Walter C. Ihejirika, *From Catholicism to Pentecostalism: The Role Nigeria TelEvangelists in Religious Conversion* (Port Harcourt: University of Port Harcourt Press, 2006).

religious beliefs and religious practice and religious praxis introduced by new religious movements. Pentecostalism and its media practices, which have attracted the most attention in this field, provide a good deal of evidence to illustrate the trend toward socio-cultural convergence.[60]

Ihejirika stresses that studies in religion and media in Africa have underscored the capacity of Pentecostalism to blend central religious paradigms and the demands of modern urbanization in order to attract adherents to itself. He concludes that the phenomenal growth of Pentecostal Christianity cannot be divorced from its ability to converge essential elements of the traditional religious beliefs and praxis in its theology and media. The table below captures Ihejirika's argument succinctly[61]:

S/No	African Religious Root-Paradigm	Elements of the Pentecostal Theology
1.	Expectations of power to emanate from religious forms.	Belief in a more powerful God. Strong emphasis on miraculous intervention in people's lives.
2	Religious power for providing children, health and wealth (resort to charms, ritual sacrifices, etc.).	Preaching of "Prosperity Theology". Strong emphasis on miraculous interventions in people's lives.

---

[60] Ihejirika, 'Research on Media, Religion and Culture in Africa,' 38-9.
[61] Ihejirika, *From Catholicism to Pentecostalism*, 112.

3.	Attribution of misfortunes to evil forces/evil person (resort to traditional medicine man)	Emphasis on the power of the devil and evil spirits to harm human beings. Ritual deliverance as remedy to evil attacks.
4.	Personal and collective sin as important causes of misfortunes.	Public confession and being "born again" as necessary for receiving God's blessings.
5.	Causality explained by appeal to gods and forces rather than to empirical factors.	Strong emphasis on miraculous interventions in people's lives. Emphasis on the power of the devil and evil spirits to harm human beings.

Convergence theory argues that religion is a tool for the average African seeking to make sense out of the various social, political, economic and cultural challenges that the continent is faced with. In essence, 'Convergence theory establishes religious media as a central mediating factor between collective and individual identities. The central argument is that the attraction of a religious movement and its media depends, to a large extent, on their capacity to provide current symbols which resonate with the traditional cultural or religious root paradigms of the individual convert or adherent.'[62] So, one characteristic element of the convergence theory is the perpetual mediation between the old and the new with the old being the traditional religious worldviews and the new being Pentecostal-Charismatic Christianity.

In a similar vein, while critiquing the impact of Nigerian Pentecostalism, its religious functionaries and their use of media on the Nigerian society, a Nigerian scholar, Olusegun Fakoya, comments thus:

---

[62] Ihejirika, 39.

The lucrative nature of this modern day pseudo-Christianity can only be examined by the rapid nature of its spread. It is particularly endearing to many Nigerians because of its tendencies to revert to traditional means in their effort to perform miracles. Their flamboyance is another attractive feature as this is well attuned to African Psyche. Pentecostal churches and hotels compete for space in Nigeria, while cinema halls, disused warehouses, bars, brothels, and night clubs have been turned to churches. To maintain their grip on the people and assure the comfort of their profit base, these churches have been extremely creative, particularly in the use of the media, radio, television, newspaper, posters, electronic mails, and even the internet. Even the Home-video industry has been virtually taken over by the Pentecostal industry.[63]

The author acknowledges the phenomenal growth of the Pentecostal film industry in Nigeria. A large percent of Christian films produced in Nigeria are coming from the film industries whose leaders and actors are influenced by Pentecostal Christianity or are from within the Nigerian Pentecostal Christian tapestry. Fakoya's argument indirectly indicates the motives of Pentecostal leaders and their adherents for appropriating the media.

To argue that Pentecostal churches and their leaders in Nigeria use media 'to maintain their grip on the people and assure the comfort of

---

[63] Olusegun Fakoya, 'The Gospel of Materialism – Nigerian Pentecostalism and Hypocrisy,' in *NVS*, in http://www.nigeriavillagesquare.com/article/dr-olusegun-fakoya/the-gospel-of-materialism-nigerian-pentecostalism-and-hypocrisy.html, posted on August 26, 2008, Accessed on July 9, 2015.

their profit base' suggests two motives. Firstly, Fakoya is suggesting that Pentecostal pastors use media to affirm their power and propagate their influences on people. He implies that film audiences are active and that the films they watch have great influence on them. Secondly, he suggests that an additional motive of Pentecostal pastors for making films is money. This position is contestable, as no empirical study was conducted by Fakoya to substantiate his argument. Such studies are needed before a generalized opinion on their appropriating of media could be established. Be that as it may, the advancement in the appropriation of media by Pentecostals, to a large extent, made their adjustment to the lockdown of corporate worship much easier, especially when compared to other strands of Christianity in Nigeria. When it comes to the appropriation of media and information communication technology (ICT), other streams of Christianity in Nigeria have a lot to learn from the Pentecostals.

CHAPTER FIVE
ESSENTIAL ELEMENTS OF CORPORATE WORSHIP IN ECWA

COVID-19 has dealt with the world in extraordinary ways. The world has changed since the outbreak. Describing the impact of the pandemic on Nigeria's educational sector, Professor Olugbemiro Jegede aptly explained that:

> The situation which has led to the closures of all educational institutions in Nigeria is unprecedented, was never in the wildest dream of anybody and has taken everybody by surprise. It was least expected and along with all that is going on with the COVID-19 situation; issues are affecting many

other sectors just as it is affecting education. The health, economic, political, socio-cultural, religious, manufacturing, transportation, oil and gas, communication and many other sectors have been affected.[1]

The scope of the impact of coronavirus has touched on all aspects of our collective existence and society. 'As has been severally established by experts, COVID-19 is the worst health crisis of the modern world.'[2] According to Jegede, 'Its effects has been massive, disruptive and destructive.'[3] Just as with other sectors, the impact has been disastrous on religion. This chapter concerns itself with how the coronavirus pandemic has disrupted the traditional configuration and practice of evangelical Christianity in Africa. Our primary concern in this book is to examine the effects of coronavirus' lockdown and social distancing with how church is done in ECWA. But before we do that, it is germane that we first and foremost describe the mode and essential elements of corporate worship in ECWA. These will serve as the templates against the parameters for measuring the effects of the coronavirus lockdown on the way church is handled in the denomination.

---

[1] Olugemiro Jegede, 'COVID-19: ODeL Will Change World's Landscape of Teaching, Learning' in *Thisday*: <u>https://www.thisdaylive.com/index.php/2020/04/08/covid-19-odel-will-change-worlds-landscape-of-teaching-learning/</u> Posted on April 8, 2020, Accessed on April 9, 2020. Olugemiro Jegede was an emeritus professor of National Open University of Nigeria and foundation vice-chancellor of the institution.

[2] Ibid.

[3] Ibid.

Mode of Worship in ECWA

Corporate worship occupies a prime place in the operations of ECWA. The denomination guards its mode of worship jealously. The identity of ECWA is entrenched and more obvious in its mode of corporate worship than any other aspect of the denomination's operations. As it is the case with other historic mission churches, the mode of worship in ECWA is *traditional*. In a traditional mode of worship, emphasis is on reverencing God through orderliness and members maintaining postures of solemnity while the corporate worship lasts.[4] In this kind of worship, it is expected that the attention of congregants is directed only towards God. Ideally, reverence for God, orderliness and sobriety should be the central goals of any given worship service in church. This tradition is not peculiar to ECWA. However, the difference comes in the ways that both the clergy and laity express themselves during corporate worship. Unlike the practice in Pentecostal denominations where people are *free* to express their *charisma* during corporate worship, 'participation of the congregation in worship is controlled' in ECWA.[5]

This *control* is seen from the beginning of the corporate worship till the end. For instance, in ECWA, clergies are expected to pay keen attention to their appearances, languages and postures during corporate worship. These qualities are also required of them outside the pulpit. Congregants expect their clergies to display spirituality, maturity, respectability and mastery of their responsibilities always, but especially while in the pulpit to lead others in worship. Below are some of the ways congregation in worship is controlled in ECWA.

---

[4] Deji Aiyegbonyin and Emiola Nihinlola, 'Pentecostalism and the Nigerian Baptist Convention Churches: The Way Forward' in *Ogbomosho Journal of Theology*, Vol. XIII (2) 2008, 221. (211-234).

[5] Ibid.

Some of the thoughts expressed below came from interaction with Deji Aiyegboyin and Emiola Nihinlola's intervention on a similar subject:

1. **Bulletins:** Most local churches use bulletins which are strictly adhered to in the course of the worship service.

2. **Service leadership:** In every corporate worship in ECWA, a service leader is appointed to provide complimentary leadership oversights alongside the pastors while the service lasts. In other words, the service leader leads the congregation through the predetermined features of a given service under the leadership and supervision of the local church pastor. Usually, a service leader is not appointed to undertake this sacred responsibility unless he is known by the pastor to have good Christian testimony and be familiar with the doctrines and practices of ECWA. This is considered important for quality control purposes.

3. **Congregational Prayer:** Usually, 'one person at a time is asked to pray aloud while the other members of the congregation say "Amen" at intervals or once at the end of the prayer.'[6]

4. **Hymn Singing:** ECWA gives preference to hymn singing than other forms of contemporary songs while in worship.

5. **Ministry of the Ushers:** Part of the many responsibilities of ushers in ECWA is to politely ensure that no one constitutes a distraction in the course of corporate worship.

---

[6] Ibid.

6. **Interjection:** 'Members of the congregation hardly interject during the service, especially while the sermon is being preached and during congregational prayer.'[7] Even children are taught to embed this value, right from their young age.

7. **Uniformity:** ECWA pastors are trained and are required to ensure uniformity in the mode of worship throughout the local church network.

Mode of worship is one of the ways Evangelicals in historic mainline churches distinguish themselves from their Pentecostal counterparts. In this vein, ECWA encourages leaders of its local churches to be on guard against unhealthy charismatic manifestations during corporate worship. Rather than putting emphasis on charismatic expressions, ECWA teaches that its members should focus 'on prayers, Bible studies, bearing fruit of the Spirit, evangelism and missions.'[8] Obviously, there is a difference between this mode of worship and the contemporary mode of worship common in Pentecostal churches. Common practices in corporate worship among Pentecostals, according to Silent Ajoku are 'Emotionalism; ecstaticism; movement in prayer; use of commanding words in prayers; violent prayers; war-oriented and chanted songs, speaking in tongues; preacher's charismatism; sowing of seeds; pushing down of miracle recipients and extreme emphasis on miracles, to list just a few.'[9] These practices are viewed by traditionalists as

---

[7] Deji Aiyegbonyin and Emiola Nihinlola.
[8] *ECWA Minister's Handbook*, 26.
[9] Silent Aduche Frank Ajoku, 'The Effects of Worship Practices in Pentecostal Church on Work Ethics in Africa' in *Ogbomosho Journal of Theology*, Vol. XIII (2) 2008, 206-20. (200-212).

having the tendency to unsettle corporate worship services, thereby dishonoring God.

Today, there is a growing departure from certain practices of orthodoxy in ECWA. Many factors are responsible for this. One such factors is the contact of and influence of Pentecostal Christianity on African society generally. According to Moses Audi, 'Every church has, or is expected to have, or manifest a level of *Charisma*.'[10] But it becomes a concern when the focus of corporate worship is on the manifestation of *grace* gifts rather than the giver of the gifts. The subtle and gradual entrance of these practices into ECWA is partly responsible for the distortion of ECWA traditional mode of worship. ECWA's mode of worship has been viewed as one of the factors responsible for the migration and emigration of youths from and into ECWA.

In view of these realities, is it proper to completely abandon the mode of worship that has been of help to many in their faith over many generations in the name of Charismatism? But for how long would ECWA look away from its pastors and members who seem to appreciate, appropriate and are manifesting extreme Charismatic tendencies during corporate worship? What should be done about pastors and members who love and uphold ECWA's mode of worship but would also appreciate blending it with some uncompromising elements of contemporary style of worship associated with Pentecostalism? Is a middle position needful and possible? A middle position is what, I presume, John Stott referred to as *Contemporary Christianity*.[11] According to him, 'To be a contemporary Christian is to ensure that our present is enriched to the fullest possible extent both by our knowledge of the past and by our expectation of the

---

[10] Moses Audi, 'Charismatic and Pentecostal Practices: An Introduction' in *Ogbomosho Journal of Theology*, Vol. XIII (2) 2008, VI. (VI-VIII).

[11] John Stott, *The Contemporary Christian* (Leicester, UK: 2004), 11.

future' (Revelation 1:8; Hebrews 13:8). These issues have raised mixed feelings and reactions among the stakeholders of ECWA over many years. Therefore, fresh investigations and interventions are required in order to chart a way forward for the denomination.

Essential Elements of Corporate Worship in ECWA

Essential elements are aspects of corporate worship in ECWA that cannot be removed or compromised. No matter the brevity of the length of corporate worship in ECWA, all the elements to be discussed are expected to be present and are essential. The only exception to these is the Holy Communion. In ECWA, the Holy Communion is more infrequent when compared to other features of corporate worship.

According to Tokunboh Adeyemo, 'Biblical worship is rooted in redemption, relationship and representation.' All three are included in Christ's definition: 'God is Spirit, and his worshippers must worship in spirit and in truth' (John 4:24, NIV).[12] The John 4:24 worship reveals the limitedness of God– our object of worship. God is Spirit and those who must worship him should connect with him spiritually. Worshippers need not be confined to a physical sacred space before they can connect with God. Whether worship is being done in the privacy of our rooms or in the sacred public worship centers, being in the spirit is the link that connects worshippers with God.

The fellowship of believers in the worship of God is central to the establishment and mission of the church in all generations. Public worship is an indispensable part of the Christian faith and

---

[12] Tokunboh Adeyemo, 'Worship and Praise' in *Africa Bible Commentary* (Nairobi: WordAlive Publishers, 2006), 251.

experience. Although, in Evangelical Christianity, individual Christians are expected to personally take responsibility for their own growth. Individual believers are expected to give equal priority to fellowshipping with other members of the family of faith (Hebrews 10:25). This is known in Greek as *Koinonia,* which means having a close bond and communion or fellowship with one or more people. This implies that an individual's spiritual growth is partly dependent on fellowship with others. All believers according to Stanley Grenz, 'need the encouragement and admonition that they receive from one another.'[13] Thus, it is a two-way approach to spiritual growth. An individual needs to fellowship with other believers in order to grow properly and normally. The church is the assembly of individual Christians coming together as one big family. Other brethren in church also need the fruits of the lives and ministries of individual Christians in order for them to grow in depth, width and to fulfil their God-given mandates on earth. Grenz stressed this fact when he explained:

> Like other emphases of evangelical spirituality, this acknowledgement of a group dependency has ramifications for our understanding of the church. The local congregation is to be an encouraging, supporting, admonishing community. Further, each member of the fellowship is to join with the others, becoming personally involved in the corporate task. We are called together not only to worship but also to enter into each other's lives and thereby foster and participate in community life, which is the essence of the ethos of the local congregation. The principle that individual believers need the resources of the

---

[13] Stanley J. Grenz, 54.

group results in a corresponding and typically evangelical emphasis on church attendance. We ought to be present for corporate church events. But the purpose lying behind this emphasis differs from that of liturgical churches. We do not tend to view attendance at the church functions as a means of grace. Instead of an automatic channel of grace, the gathered community is a vehicle of instruction and encouragement.[14]

From Grenz's submission above, two thoughts are essential for our emphasis. Firstly, Evangelical spirituality promotes the integration of individual Christians into the church life. Secondly, the church is the instructional resource centre for the continued growth of individual Christians and so, being involved in its growth initiatives is non-negotiable for believers. This Evangelical position has its roots in the Bible. But besides the benefits, believers are expected to worship in order to give reverence to God. If worship 'is the practice of showing respect for God'[15]; then its primary purpose would be to reference God.

ECWA as an evangelical denomination gives premium priority to public worship. In its *Minister's Handbook*, ECWA explains that, 'In worship, we seek to ascribe worth, honour, glory and majesty to God Almighty.'[16] In order to achieve this, ECWA liturgy is built on a tradition of simple but highly reverent public worship. In my observation, I believe there are five essential elements of public worship in ECWA and they are: proclamation of the Word of God;

---

[14] Ibid.

[15] A.S. Horby, 'Worship' in Oxford Advanced Learner's Dictionary of Current English (Oxford: Oxford University Press, 2000), 1379.

[16] 'Worship Service' in *ECWA Minister's Handbook* (Jos: Challenge Press, 2002), 24.

prayer, music, Christian giving and Holy Communion. Let us now proceed to treating the elements one after the other.

Proclamation of the Word of God

Of the five essential elements of public worship in ECWA, none is as important as the preaching and teaching of the Word of God. ECWA confirm this in the *Minister's Handbook:* 'The most significant part of our church service is the sermon, therefore, it must come not later than the halfway in the period of the worship service and should be given at least thirty minutes.'[17] 'Significance' according to ECWA's position can be measured by the position and amount of time allocated to the proclamation of the Word in a worship service. A separate study would be needed to determine the appropriateness and effectiveness of the average time recommended by ECWA for sermon delivery. The recommendation on time is only a guideline and so, preachers are not necessarily expected to strictly adhere to it. Preachers are expected to use their discretions in the management of time depending on their contexts and the nature of services they are leading. Besides, there are additional practices that affirm the priority that ECWA gives to the proclamation of the Word of God.

Now, we come to the content and object of the proclamation itself. 'The aim of worship is to help direct the attention of worshippers to Jesus Christ, the Lord who is the Object of worship, praise and adoration.'[18] In every public worship, ECWA preachers are expected to proclaim the lordship of Jesus and show believers how to walk and work for him. This particular agenda has two ends in mind – the discipleship of believers and the evangelization of individuals who

---

[17] 'Worship Service' in *ECWA Minister's Handbook* (Jos: Challenge Press, 2002), 25.
[18] Ibid., 24.

come to church but are yet to have a salvation encounter with Jesus. Preachers are therefore not expected to seek attention for themselves but for Christ. Is that not what true discipleship entails?

According to Tokunboh Adeyemo, 'Faithful disciples are characterized by qualities such as abiding in Jesus' word, steadfast faith in him, loyalty to him, love for one another, walking in the light, bearing fruit and humble service to one another (John 8:31-36; 13:34-35). Discipleship also requires obedience to his commands (Luke 6:46), specifically the commands to love God and our neighbors and make disciples of all nations (Matthew 22: 37-39; 28:18-20).'[19] Discipleship is a process, and it can take place and be sustained in an atmosphere where sound biblical preaching thrives. Only thoroughly breed believers can contribute to the growth of the local church where they are located. ECWA realizes this and that is why preaching the Word of God is handled seriously. Apart from the usual Sunday worship services, on the average, there are midweek follow-up services where the Word of God is taught on a weekly basis in every registered local church in ECWA. This mission is channeled through the Men, Women and Youth Fellowship agencies of the denomination.

One additional importance of the proclamation of the Word of God in ECWA is the evangelization of unbelievers within the local church context. This factor is crucial for all public worship services in ECWA. The denomination sees it as an opportunity to reach the unsaved with the gospel. In most cases, the name of a thing has a lot to with its nature. This is also true of the Evangelical Church Winning All (ECWA). Thus, the name of the denomination portrays the evangelical nature of the mission. But it goes beyond just bearing

---

[19] Tokunboh Adeyemo, 'Discipleship' in *Africa Bible Commentary* (Nairobi: WordAlive Publishers, 2006), 1223.

the name the *Evangelical,* ECWA does strongly believe in and is involved in the evangelization of unsaved souls, both within and outside the local church setting. Historically, the primary aim of the first set of its founding missionaries that came to Africa and through whose hands the church was established was evangelism. Cornelius Olowola corroborated that when he declared:

> History has it that Evangelism was one of the priorities of ECWA. Before the church was registered, an Evangelistic Mission was formed named African Missionary Society (AMS). Pastors who felt called were posted to Dahomey (now Benin Republic) and other places. The AMS of those days is now the Evangelical Missionary Society of ECWA today. The mission society has more than one thousand missionaries serving in different parts of the country (Nigeria) and overseas.[20]

The demography cited above has changed significantly almost twenty years later. ECWA now has about two thousand missionaries serving in Nigeria and overseas.[21] The EMS of ECWA is one of the most organized mission agencies in the contemporary global church. In the year 2018, ECWA established a television station in its headquarters at Jos, Plateau State of Nigeria. In his speech at the launch of the TV station, the then ECWA President Rev. Dr. Jeremiah Gado submitted that:

---

[20] Cornelius A. Olowola, 'ECWA President's Address to the Participants of ECWA South-West Zonal Consultative Forum', at Ilorin, October 19, 2002, 2.

[21] Allan L. Effa, 'Releasing the Trigger: The Nigerian Factor in Global Christianity' in *International Bulletin of Missionary Research,* Vol. 37, No. 4, (October 2013), 214-215. (214-218).

SIM-ECWA is among the first missionary outfits to use modern media to reach out with the good news of salvation, teachings about Christian faith and Christian living in Africa. The addition of ECWA TV to the existing Radio ELWA and *Today's Challenge Magazine* makes it possible for ECWA to explore a broad spectrum of ministries designed to provide platforms for Christians within and outside ECWA to proclaim the gospel of God's kingdom to the whole world. Through ECWA TV, God's eternal love to the world would be proclaimed in a world filled with prejudice, hate, conflicts and confusion. Another focus of ECWA TV is to address the daily challenges Christians and humanity face in a dynamic world that presents humanity with more choice of evil than godly standards.[22]

African Church historian and theologian Ogbu Kalu had earlier confirmed Radio ELWA as the earliest Evangelical modern media ministry to have his inroads to Africa. According to Kalu, "Most West Africans listened to the Christian broadcast from Eternal Love Will Win All–ELWWA (which later became Eternal Love Winning All–ELWA) Radio, Monrovia, founded in 1954 by three young Evangelicals from Wheaton, Illinois: William Watkins, Abe Thiessen and Merle Steely. The success of this tropicalizing of the radio ministry was due to the wartime advances in high frequency transmission, availability of surplus military equipment . . . The history of Radio ELWA still needs to be written as the backdrop to

---

[22] 'ECWA Church Lunches TV Station' in *The Nation*:https://thenationonlineng.net/ecwa-church-lunches-tv-station/ Posted on June 3, 2018, Accessed April 13, 2020.

the excitement of 1980s televangelism.'[23] All these efforts stress the centrality of evangelism and missionary involvement to ECWA.

Further, the training of pastoral leaders, the preachers of the gospel and leaders of the local church is central to the vision and mission of ECWA. Apart from the non-negotiable requirement of being called by God to provide leadership to the church, pastors are also required to possess a certain level of formal theological training and must be willing to serve full-time before they can assume the pastoral duties in any of the ECWA local church networks. For the sake of effectiveness and fruitfulness, there are other basic qualifications required of the pastor, but this is beyond the immediate scope of this study. While theological education is not a full insulation against propagation of misleading theologies and doctrines, ECWA believes that the possession of the same can serve to reduce the danger of heretical teaching from pastors to their members.

ECWA upholds the supremacy of the Bible. Interpreters of the Bible are expected to hold the same view by preaching sound biblical doctrines. The singular goal of ECWA is to glorify God, and one of its objectives for achieving this is to 'preach and teach the Holy Bible as the inspired and infallible Word of God.'[24] A Pastor is expected to have undergone a minimum of three years of theological training in an approved theological institution before he can be employed and licensed to undertake ministry in ECWA. Additionally, a minimum of *Bachelor's Degree in Theology* is required to hold any position reserved for the clergy in Local Church Council (LCC), District Church Council (DCC) and the General Church Council (GCC).[25] These requirement are indicators of the importance that ECWA

---

[23] Ogbu Kalu, *African Pentecostalism* (Oxford: Oxford University Press, 2008), 106.

[24] Constitution of the Evangelical Church Winning All: As Amended 2019 (Jos: ECWA Headquarters, 2019), 2.

[25] Ibid., 12, 41.

attaches to the proclamation of sound doctrine. To be found guilty of heretical teaching and tendency is one of the misconducts that attracts the severest form of discipline in ECWA, excommunication. What is the mission of the church on earth? If the church 'is a vehicle of instruction and encouragement to believers', then preaching and teaching should not look different. Preaching that lacks integrity is one of the banes of the church in Africa. In a separate intervention, I argued that lack of sound biblical teachings and 'the growing breed of avaricious pastors is one of the major factors undermining the impact of the Christian message in the public sphere in Africa.'[26] In a recent book published by one of the most revered pioneers of the Scripture Union (SU) in Nigeria, Emmanuel Oladipo reveals that it is possible to lead a life of integrity in context where corruption prevails. In the book *Exemplary Christians in the Nigerian Public Square*[27], Oladipo gives an unbiased and compelling account of fifteen Christian couples who served in some of the highest public offices in Nigeria and left legacies of Christian integrity and exploits in the historical annals of the country. The book shows us examples of Christian men and women who were deliberate in transforming their workplace and the Nigerian public square by the quality of the lives they lived. The author shows us that living the genuine Christian life is not an impossible mission, even in Nigeria, and so, our Christianity must go beyond the four walls of the church. It is instructive to highlight that more than half of Christian couples whose lives were x-rayed by Oladipo were either members or affiliates of ECWA. While this may not be enough to adjudge the

---

[26] Moses Owojaiye, 'The Problem of False Prophets in Africa' in *Lausanne Global Analysis*, Volume 8, Issue 6 (November 2019): https://www.lausanne.org/content/lga/2019-11/problem-false-prophets-africa.

[27] Emmanuel Oladipo, *Exemplary Christians in the Nigerian Public Square* (Ibadan: BLISS International Publishing, 2018).

success of the preaching ministry of ECWA, it points to the effort of the denomination in that direction. ECWA remains one of the most influential and respected evangelical voices on the African continent, largely because of its disposition to the proclamation of the gospel and the outcome of the same in its membership and in the Nigerian public square.

Prayer

Prayer is another essential element of public worship in ECWA. Because of its nonmilitant and charismatic approach to prayer, many have erroneously stereotyped it as a prayer-less denomination. While I doubt whether any Christian can ever pray enough, that is not enough reason to accuse an individual of being prayerful or prayer-less. How should we measure prayerfulness? Is it by the mode, length or content? One of the nuggets of E.M. Bounds on the subject of prayer is worthy of note at this point. According to Bounds, "Prayer is a most serious work of our most serious years."[28] Prayer is certainly one of the core characteristics of Evangelicals. Realising this, ECWA gives precedence to prayer in its public worship services. Every meeting features four strands of congregational prayers, namely: call to worship, pastoral prayer, offertory prayer and closing prayer. There are also instances in which members are required to pray individually, even during public worship services. There must be reverence and decorum while the worship service lasts, and that includes prayer sessions. ECWA promotes orderliness and reverence in its worship services, a disorderly approach to congregational prayer is unwelcomed.

---

[28] E.M. Bounds, *Power Through Prayer* (Hobe Sound: Gospel Publishing Mission, 2000), 22.

The slogan of the founding fathers of ECWA was, 'SIM by prayer'. Thus, prayer is the very nature of the denomination. SIM (Serving in Mission) depends on prayer as a means of softening people's hearts to the message of salvation, providing resources, protection and direction. The ministry emphasizes the importance of prayer as central to having breakthroughs in missionary involvements for the salvation of the unsaved and for the growth and revival of the global church.[29] The impact of prayer could be confirmed in the breakthroughs that the denomination has witnessed so far in its missionary efforts in its 125 years of existence.

Was it not prayer that won the legal battle between ECWA Productions Limited (EPL), the publisher of *Today's Challenge* and the Ancient and Mystical Order Rosae Crucis (AMORC), also known as the 'The Rosicrucian Order', when the former published an expose on the latter declaring it a secret and occultic society? The libel lawsuit battle lasted for ten years from 1984 to 1994. Through prayers and the professional acumen of Barrister Wole Olufon, the Supreme Court of Nigeria *per* five justices gave a judgment in favor of EPL.[30] The leadership of ECWA has continued to establish the importance of prayer through its occasional calls for members to pray and fast on national issues. One of these issues is the incessant attacks of *Boko Haram* on Christians in Northeast Nigeria with the peak being the abduction of Leah Sharibu and other ECWA members on February 19, 2018. John Stott was right when he declared, 'Prayer is the only power which the powerless possess.'[31] As important as prayer is in public worship, ECWA promotes individual personal dependence on Christ through prayer as the necessary prerequisite to effective congregational prayer.

---

[29] 'Prayer with us' in https://www.sim.org/pray-with-us/ Accessed on April 13, 2020.
[30] See Wole Olufon, *Who is with you?* (Lagos: Shalom Holding and Ventures, 2002).
[31] John R.W. Stott, *The Message of Acts* (Leicester: Intervarsity Press, 1990), 209.

Spiritual Songs

Through music, we give reverence, praise and adoration to God. Songs are essential elements of public worship. They are inseparable features of both private and public worship, and ECWA is not an exception to this reality. Africans are known for their undying love for music, and this is partly because it helps in the expression of our day-to-day walk with Christ and his interventions, both in personal and social living. The Bible is full of examples of people who sang praises as a form of worship to God. A significant part of the Book of Psalms came from David's personal experiences with God. Christians are even admonished to *'Speak to one another with psalms, hymns and spiritual songs. Sing and make music in your heart to the Lord...'* (Ephesians 5:19, NIV). The songs should be biblically sound. Like the proclamation of the Word of God, spiritual songs serve many purposes, ranging from worship of God, evangelism and instructional for Christian living as a means of advocacy, even in the public square and for spiritual warfare.

Spiritual songs in ECWA come in two strands–contemporary songs and classical hymns. Let me address the role of contemporary songs in public worship in ECWA, especially when it comes to evangelism. I consider it a method of evangelism in ECWA–Music Evangelism. This means reaching unbelieving persons through music. ECWA is known in the body of Christ in Nigeria for its endowment in gospel music. This gift includes the ability to present biblically sound songs inspiring and compelling enough to attract unbelievers to Christ through the help of the Holy Spirit. Many unbelievers have been won to Christ through this avenue. Believers in Christ alike have experienced personal seasons of revival in their walk with Christ through spiritual songs. ECWA's special endowment in spiritual songs have not only won many to Christ, it has served to attract and retain many to membership.

Besides the regular Sunday services where these songs form a major part of public worship, this method of evangelism is done by organized live musical concerts with the purpose of strengthening the faith of believers and attracting unbelievers to Christ. The songs are sometimes transmitted on Radio ELWA and ECWA TV to serve the same purposes. They are attractive, not just because of the anointing of the Holy Spirit on them, but also because they are largely sang in various Nigerian indigenous languages, depending on the context where such ministration take place. The Annual Festival of Gospel Songs (FESTIGOS) organized in many locations in Nigeria are typical examples of this type of Evangelism. The annual services of songs organized by different singing groups in the local church networks in ECWA (e.g., Main, Men, Women, Youth, English and Children Choirs) are all aimed at the singular purpose of winning souls. In a nutshell, spiritual songs serve as one of the most powerful and effective methods of evangelism and discipleship in public worship in ECWA. This includes the importance of hymns in worship in ECWA. Hymn singing is the most pronounced form of spiritual songs in public worship in ECWA.

Holy Communion

Unlike liturgical churches where Holy Communion is served on a more frequent basis, the service is more often than not a once a month or quarterly experience within the ECWA.[32] That is not to say that this sacred aspect of public worship is less important in ECWA. ECWA holds that the Holy Communion is one of the ordinances of the church commanded by the Lord Jesus in Luke 22:19-20 and Matthew 26:26-28 and affirmed by the Apostle Paul in

---

[32] 'Holy Communion Service' in *ECWA Minister's Handbook*, 77.

1 Corinthians 11:23–25 and 10:16–17. As such, heeding the command is far more important than the frequency of participation.

The doctrinal position of ECWA on the Holy Communion stresses its importance in ECWA. The ECWA Minister's Handbook states:

> ECWA believe that bread and wine which are taken at the Lord's Supper table do not change into actual flesh and blood of the Lord. We do not believe that the partaking of the elements bestows any grace upon the participant. The blessing is in the attitude of the heart of the one who takes it. The Christian sets his heart again to think more about Christ and His atoning work. The blessing also comes as the partaker proclaims the death of Christ to the world in word and deed until He comes. While this ordinance also is not necessary for salvation it is worthwhile for the Christian to partake of it since Christ commanded it. We believe that it is the duty of the partaker to examine himself to see whether he is approaching the table with a clean heart. It is an hour for the Christian to come to himself and search his heart and also to get right with God (Psalm 139: 23, 24). We expect all the partakers of the Lord's Supper to have placed their faith in the Lord Jesus Christ and to have been baptized, and to be in good standing... [33]

The quote above is self-explanatory. While born-again visitors and attendees are not banned from participating, only the

---

[33] Ibid, 77-8.

registered members have the *bona fide* right of participating in Holy Communion in ECWA.[34]

Holy Communion is one of the essential elements of public worship in ECWA for three important reasons. First, it was commanded by the Lord Jesus Christ. Second, it reminds the believer of his covenant relationship with Jesus Christ. The need to always be reminded and to continually lead a worthy life on earth cannot be overstated. Finally, this is one aspect of ECWA's liturgy that non-clergy members cannot undertake privately or personally. In other words, only accredited pastors have the right to administer Holy Communion in the denomination. This is due to the importance and the sacredness of the service to the denomination[35] while ordination

---

[34] To be a registered member of ECWA, one must have been: (i) born again; (ii) must have gone through ECWA's Baptismal Class; (iii) must have gone through pre-baptismal interview; (iv) must have had water baptism by immersion; and (v) must have publicly recited the Apostle's Creed on the ECWA Membership form in a Baptismal and Membership Intake Service where new members partake in Holy Communion and are publicly introduced to congregants in that particular worship service in a duly constituted local church (See *Constitution of the ECWA-As Amended 2019*, 11).

[35] An accredited pastor is a members of the clergy in ECWA who have attained a minimum height of a licentiate in him ministry with ECWA. 'To be licensed, an ECWA employee or any ECWA member shall be approved by the ECWA Executive and shall be required to fulfill the following conditions: (a) satisfy the requirements in 1 Timothy 3:1-7 and Titus 1:6-9; (b)have spent five years in ECWA employment; (c) undergo Bible training in any ECWA approved institution for a minimum of (3) years; (d) in addition to [b] above, sit and pass ECWA doctrinal examination, if the institution was non-ECWA; undergo licensing and induction course, organized by ECWA headquarters and (f) sit and pass Part I examination on the following documents: (i) ECWA Constitution; (ii) ECWA Bye-Laws; (iii) Minister's Handbook; (iv) SIM/ECWA History; (v) ECWA Manual; (vi) ECWA Financial Policy and Guidelines; (vii) ECWA Condition of Service and (viii) Other ECWA documents' (see Bye-Laws of ECWA-As Amended 2019), 41-2. A licensed pastor in ECWA has the authority to conduct and official certain ministerial function in ECWA part of which administering Holy Communion.

is the highest, pastors who have not attained that height in ECWA are expected to wait on the leadership of those around them who have been empowered to undertake such ministries.

Christian Giving

The subject of Christian giving, in particular as it relates to tithing, has triggered controversy in Nigeria in recent years. The debate was particularly more pronounced within the Pentecostal-Charismatic circles, as it concerns the disposition of some Pentecostal-Charismatic denominational leaders on the subject of tithing. This book is not an attempt to resolve the tension but to highlight the interest of Christians in this topic.

Giving is an integral part of worship. It is an act of worship to God (2 Corinthians 8:5; Matthew 2:11), and that is why its place in public worship is inevitable. Giving reveals believers' level of love, obedience, dedication, loyalty and maturity in Christ. This act of worship is rooted in the Bible. The Bible instructs that every believer is a steward of everything possessed. 'Each one should whatever gift he has received to serve others, faithfully administering God's grace in its various forms' (1Peter 4:10, NIV). Another Scripture that teaches that believers are stewards of God's resources in their custody is 1 Chronicles 29:14, and James 1:17. 1 Chronicles 29:14 states, '. . . Everything comes from you, and we have given you only what comes from your hand' (NIV). A steward is one who manages, administers and takes care of that which belongs to another. God is the source of man's blessedness, and he expects us to be stewards of all he has given to us.

God is the believer's perfect model for giving. Examples of God's matchless generosity is scattered across the Bible. But the chief of them all is the sacrificial giving of Jesus for the salvation and redemption of humankind (John 3:16 Romans 8:31-32). God expects every believer to demonstrate this attribute in Christian living. This should enable believers have the right attitude to life as well as human possessions. No Christian is too poor to give (1 Kings 17:7-16; Luke 21:1-4). The Bible teaches that every Christian should give generously (Mark 14: 3-19), cheerfully (2 Corinthians 9:7), regularly (2 Corinthians 8:11), voluntarily (Exodus 35:21, 26, 29, 36) and (2 Corinthians 9:7), excellently (2 Corinthians 8:7), sacrificially (2 Corinthians 8:2-3) and quietly (Matthew 6:1-4). Believers honor God when they give to his mission (2 Corinthians 9:7) and they get blessed for being involved in this ministry while on earth (2 Corinthians 9:8, Galatians 6:7-8, Psalm 112:9 and Proverbs 22:9). The ultimate reward for our giving awaits us at the presence of God in Heaven (2 Corinthians 5:10).

Precipitated on the biblical positions highlighted above, ECWA teaches and encourages its members to the blessedness of Christian giving by proving participatory opportunities for them through public worship. Whereas Christian giving should be private, providing opportunity through public worship implies giving to God through his established institution – the church. As stated in its constitution, 'ECWA's sources of income come from offering, tithing, special fundraising, freewill donations, grants or gifts and dues.'[36] By implication, ECWA operates and funds its mission through proceeds from the aforementioned sources.

Finances are particularly important for the evangelistic, discipleship and activistic ministries of the church. We see the importance of this even in the early church. The Bible states in Acts 4:34-35 that, '. . . There were no needy persons among them. For from time to time those who owned land or houses sold them,

---

[36] *Constitution of the Evangelical Church Winning All - As Amended 2019*, 15.

brought the money from the sales and put it at the apostles' feet, and it was distributed to anyone who had need.' (NIV). Fundraising may not be done today exactly the way it was done in the early church. You will recall that some fundraising methods were later corrupted by Satan through Ananias and Sapphira (Acts 5:1-11). However, the principle behind the practice remains an example for the contemporary church to emulate. While commenting on the place of Christian giving in the early church in Acts 4: 1-47, John Stott explained that, 'Christian fellowship is Christian caring, and Christian caring is Christian sharing.'[37] Quoting Chrysostom's explanation of Acts 4:34-35, John Stott stressed that:

> This was an angelic commonwealth, not to call anything of theirs their own. Forthwith the root of evils was cut out . . . None reproached, none envied, none grudged; no pride, no contempt was there... The poor man knew no shame, the rich no haughtiness. So we must not evade the challenge of these verses. That we have hundreds of thousands of destitute brothers and sisters is a standing rebuke to us who are more affluent. It is part of the responsibility of Spirit-filled believers to alleviate need and abolish destitution in the new community of Jesus.[38]

Christian giving through public worship is therefore one of the ways ECWA is able to carry its responsibility to God, its members and to the general public. Even though ECWA understands the importance of money to the fulfillment of its mission, it tries to

---

[37] John R.W. Stott, *The Message of Acts*, 84.
[38] Ibid.

maintain a biblical and easygoing approach to Christian giving. Emphasis is placed on willful and cheerful giving. ECWA encourages its members to give freely by promoting the culture of financial transparency, propriety and accountability.[39]

As I round off this chapter, I would like to submit that Evangelical Christianity has three ends in mind. These four ends are intertwined, interdependent and interrelated. First, it focuses on personal piety of individual believers. Second, it focuses on the maintenance of communal bond through regular fellowship with other brethren. Third, it concerns itself with societal transformation through evangelistic and activistic involvements. Thus each believer is expected to be involved both individually and collectively in this quadrilateral mission of the church. The essence of these is so believers can ultimately succeed in their pursuit of possessing a final habitation with God in Heaven. This can only be achieved by being born-again and through sustained walk with and work for Christ while here on earth. ECWA, through its essential elements of public worship, serve to support believers in attaining these ends.

---

[39] See *Constitution of the Evangelical Church Winning All-As Amended 2019*, 15, 16, 18 and 19.

CHAPTER SIX
CORONAVIRUS LOCKDOWN AND CORPORATE WORSHIP IN ECWA

The term *lockdown* is not a new word in the English vocabulary but has recently gained massive prominence during the COVID-19 worldwide lockdowns. According to the Merriam-Webster Dictionary, 'Lockdown is an emergency measure or condition in which people are temporarily prevented from entering or leaving a restricted area or building (such as a school) during a threat of danger.'[1] In this case, COVID-19, it is the partial or total prevention of free human movements from one location to another in order to contain and prevent human-to-human infection. The lockdown was

---

[1] 'Lockdown' in https://www.merriam-webster.com/dictionary/lockdown, Accessed on April 12, 2020.

observed in virtually all the countries of the world, and it lasted for several weeks or months depending on the contexts. During these lockdowns, local, international and national borders were closed, and only essential workers were allowed to move around. People were advised to stay at home. Some countries, states and regions of the world even promulgated laws to enforce the lockdown order, and those who broke the law are made to face the consequences.

What about *Social and Physical Distancing?* According to Layal Liverpool, 'Social distancing practices are changes in behaviour that can help stop the spread of infections. These often include curtailing social contact, work and schooling among seemingly healthy individuals, with a view to delaying transmission and reducing the size of an outbreak.'[2] Since coronavirus is a droplet borne disease, Liverpool explains further that individuals can lower the risk of infection by reducing their rate of contact with other people. Avoidance of public spaces and unnecessary social gatherings, especially events with a large number of people or crowds, will lower the chances of being exposed to coronavirus.[3] The World Health Organization recommended a distance of one to two metres between person-to-person, especially individuals coughing or sneezing, and avoidance of physical contact such as handshakes, hugs and kisses.

It is instructive to note that the issue of social distancing was responsible for the closure of all social and religious institutions across the world. The social distance measure was more pronounced during partial lockdowns. But total lockdown indicated the restriction of human movement to the barest minimum. None of the

---

[2] Layal Liverpool, 'Coronavirus: What is social distancing and do you do it?' in *NewScientist*: https://www.newscientist.com/article/2237664-coronavirus-what-is-social-distancing-and-how-do-you-do-it/ Posted on March 17, 2020, Accessed on April 12, 2020.
[3] Ibid.

measures prescribed for the prevention and containment of spread of COVID-19 has had a more adverse effect on the church than those of social distancing and total lockdown. Now, let us examine the effects of these measures on the church with specific focus on the Evangelical Church Winning All (ECWA).

Effects of COVID-19 Lockdown and Corporate Worship in ECWA

I doubt whether there is a Christian who would have envisaged that a time would come in the world that the doors of the church would be closed to corporate worship before the rapture takes place. The outbreak of coronavirus and its containment and preventive measures, such as social distancing and lockdowns, caught everyone unawares. As it is the case with all other sectors of our living, the impact of coronavirus on public worship in ECWA was unprecedented. This also accounts for why the majority of Christians cannot physically attend church services. Being involved in corporate worship is beyond a desire. It is an obligation that all believers in Christ are enjoined to observe (Hebrews 10:25). According to David Matthis, 'Corporate worship plays an indispensable role in the in rekindling our spiritual fire, and keeping it burning. Corporate worship brings together God's word, prayer, fellowship, and so makes for the greatest means of God's ongoing grace in the Christian life.'[4]

Not being able to fellowship has a huge implication on the personal life of a believer, as well as that of the church. David Robertson stresses this fact when he submits that, 'We need to consider carefully the cost of closing churches. Not the financial

---

[4] David Mathis, 'Five Benefits of Corporate Worship' in *DesiringGod*: https://www.desiringgod.org/articles/five-benefits-of-corporate-worship/

cost but rather the psychological, emotional and spiritual cost to people. There are many people for whom the weekly gathering of the Lord's people is a real strength and community for them. The mental harm caused by the fear of pandemic, and the constant 24/7 media and online hysteria should be factored in as well.'[5] The directives of the Government of the Federal Republic of Nigeria and all the federating states were binding on all the citizens of the country, and members of ECWA are not exempted from the rule. It is true that the shutdown of churches by government was necessitated by the coronavirus pandemic, and it is for the collective good of all. But it must also be stressed that the effects of the closure of churches on Christians cannot be overstated. Here are some of the ways that COVID-19 lockdown affected corporate worship in ECWA.

Corporate Worship Replaced with e-Worship

One of the major effects of coronavirus lockdown on ECWA is the sudden migration from physical corporate worship to virtual worship. The role of the media in providing a leverage for churches during this period cannot be overemphasized. The appropriation of media in this sense include the use of TV, radio and social media. For instance, the leadership of ECWA was able to transmit through ECWA TV every Sunday. ECWA members who could not join the e-worship via the TV also took advantage of their local church services transmitted

---

[5] David Robertson, 'What is the Impact of Churches Closing Because of Coronavirus?' in *Christianity Today*: https://www.christianitytoday.com/article/what-is-the-impact-of-churches-closing-because-of-coronavirus/134477.htm/ Posted on March 18, 2020, Accessed on April 16, 2020.

through the social media. As good as these palliative measures were, they came with their own unique challenges.

Disparity in the Reach of the Targeted Audience Members

Let me state here that this book does not concern itself with scholarly debates on the effects of the media on its audience members. One of the unique characteristics of both traditional and modern media is its capacity to reach a wide range of people within a shorter period of time. This ability is captured in the mission statement of ECWA TV: 'Reaching out to the world through media by preaching, teaching and inspiring, winning all for Christ Jesus and raising a godly generation.'[6] Pastors who made use of TV and social media had dual experiences in relation to the disparity in the reach of their media platforms. Some were able to reach far more people than they would incorporate worship services. This reach cuts across age, gender, race, and ethnicity, theological, doctrinal and denominational differences. Such was the experience of a local church in the United Kingdom. According to a BBC report, 'A virtual congregation set up during the coronavirus lockdown has caused an Edinburgh church's number to be eight times their normal size... The Scottish Episcopal Church, which has a predominantly young congregation of about 1,000, normally sees between 500 and 600 people at Sunday service. However on Sunday 22 March [2020], its virtual service was watched live 4,300 times giving a reach of more than 8000'[7]

---

[6] 'ECWA TV Africa: Our Core Values and Beliefs' in *ECWA TV*: http://ecwatv.org/about-us/ Accessed on April 16, 2020.

[7] Angie Brown, 'Edinburgh Church Congregation Grows under Lockdown' in BBC News: https://www.bbc.com/news/uk-scotland-edinburgh-east-fife-52262025/ Posted April 12, 2020, Accessed on April 16, 2020.

This probably would be the experience in churches situated in urban contexts, especially if these churches are famous for something unique in their localities. Having a famous preacher or Bible teacher, choir or a unique mode of worship could be an added advantage. But the story was different for others. The factors behind this were nuanced, complex and complicated, ranging from finances, accessibility, and quality of production and content of media texts. To a large extent, the strength of the mass media is also its weakness. Because it is a virtual worship, the pastor has no opportunity to address individuals. This breeds a mental and emotional disconnect between worship leaders and their targeted audience members. And this, by implication, may affect the way the content of e-worship is transmitted, received and processed.

Traditional and Social Media, the Rural Poor, and Aged

There also exists a high level of disparity. While the urban, rich churches succeeded in immediately migrating to online services, the church neglected an entire demography. What happened to the rural, poor and aged members of the church? What would be the implication of this on the post-COVID19 era of the church? This is a pressing reality in Africa. Nigeria has one of the most vibrant telecommunications industries in the world. According to a report credited to *Business Day*:

> In the first two quarters of 2019, the ICT sector recorded growth in the number of active voice subscribers . . . It grew by 7.21[%] . . . and 7.41[%] . . . in the first quarter (Q1) and the second quarter (Q2) 2019 respectively compared to the 162.03 million subscribers in Q4 2018. Telecoms data from the National Bureau of Statistics were active on voice in

Q1 2019; representing 0.19 per cent increase from Q1 2019. The Q2 subscriber base also accounted for over 87 per cent penetration rate. The analysis of the active internet subscription in the review period showed that the sector recorded 18.51[%] . . . and 12.36[%] . . . increase from Q4 2018 subscriber base 103.51 million to 122.67 million active internet subscribers in Q2 2019 respectively. However, the number of active internet subscribers was down by 5.19 per cent from Q1 to Q2 in 2019.[8]

The analyses above reveals that in the first quarter of 2019, Nigeria had 170 million mobile phone subscribers. This was significant for a country with a population of about 200 million people. Almost every Nigerian now knows the value of owning a mobile phone, at least when it comes to communication and commercial services. This perhaps is accountable for the number of voice subscribers recorded in Nigeria in 2019. The story is different when it comes to internet services. In the year under review, about 80 million Nigerians were out of the active internet subscribers' radar. This is very significant. While it is true that the statistics cited above are not up to date, the difference between when the statistics were released and now could not be significantly different. What happens to the remaining 80 million people? This includes the aged or people living in poor, rural contexts who probably do not understand the purpose of the internet or may not have financial means to service it.

Could a sizeable part of the Nigerian church be among the

---

[8] Ademola Asunloye, 'Spotlight on Nigeria's Telecommunications Sector' in *Business Day*: https://businessday.ng/business-economy/article/spotlight-on-nigerias-telecommunications-sector/Posted on October 24, 2019, Accessed on April 16, 2020.

uncaptured 80 million Nigerians who could not afford to subscribe to the internet? And ECWA being a denomination with massive presence in rural and semi-urban settlements in Nigeria may have a significant representation among those people. This is bearing in mind that ECWA has more than six thousand congregations scattered across Nigeria with a strength of about 10,000,000 members. With Nigeria being one of the epicenters of poverty in the world, there are many who could not even afford to own a radio or television set. To complicate the matter, some of these people are not literate enough to write or read the Bible themselves. They depend mainly on whatever they learn directly through their fellowship from the educational ministries of the church in order to advance in individual spiritual growth. Such individuals were edged out and had to spiritually fend for themselves until the post-coronavirus phase of the Church. Coronavirus lockdown in a context of abject poverty and without government palliatives further compounded the financial predicament of many of these members.

Finances and Infrequency of e-Worship

Another effect of the coronavirus lockdown on ECWA is the infrequent nature of the e-church platforms and its financial burden on the church, as well as on individual Christians. While is true that ECWA TV transmits 24/7, it does so on a frequency that makes it challenging for many Nigerians to access. Whereas private individuals have the right to own media stations in Nigeria, they can only do so when their agendum to be promoted are not religious or political. According to the National Broadcasting Commission (NBC), religious and political organizations with the sole aim of promoting religious and political contents are prohibited from consideration for the grant of a broadcasting license. This is due to the volatile political and religious tensions in many parts of the country. An alternative option for interested religious bodies is to consider free-to-air terrestrial television and an FM radio license, satellite television broadcasting services or community radio.[9] The cost of obtaining these licenses, the reach of their services and accessibility to viewers vary. ECWA, as of the time of writing this book, operates on the free-to-air terrestrial television license. Unlike public TV stations, which are free to members of the public, interested viewers of the free-to-air TV contents would have to pay an initial installation fee. As inexpensive as the installation is, there are members of the Nigerian public who cannot afford it. Besides, how convenient is it for members to worship through the TV in a country where less than 50 million households have access to television?[10]

The ball of the challenge was thrown to the court of the local church's leadership to provide creative palliatives when a significant number of their members were unable to join ECWA TV. ECWA leadership took advantage of social media platforms, such as Facebook and YouTube to reach a segment of its members who could not join via TV. There were local churches in ECWA who made separate arrangements. One of such local churches is First ECWA Church, Ilorin, Nigeria. This initiative also come with at least three challenges. First, not all ECWA local churches can afford online services. Even most of the local churches that managed to set up online services did so at the mercy of their congregants, who either sponsored the project or made private equipment available. Most of

---

[9] 'Procedure for Obtaining License' in *National Broadcasting Commission*: https://www.nbc.gov.ng/pages/licensing/ Accessed on April 16, 2020.

[10] Taiwo George, 'Only 37 Million Households in Nigeria have access to Television' in *TheCable*: https://www.thecable.ng/37-million-households-nigeria-access-television/ Posted on September 16, 2020, Accessed on April 30, 2020.

the ECWA local assemblies did not have internet infrastructure in place before the COVID-19 pandemic. This is an indication of the disposition of the denomination to internet infrastructure. Besides unaffordability of streaming online worship services to most ECWA local churches, the case is not different for most of its members. These challenges have made e-services infrequent and reduced to a once a week experience for churches that can afford it for members who, without the lockdown, would have attended an average of two to three midweek services per week. For these people, it was a big dissatisfaction to resort to a once a week online service.

Lack of Fellowship and Warmth on Social Media or TV

According to Don Whitney, 'There is an element of worship and Christianity that cannot be experienced in private worship or by watching worship. There are some graces and blessings that God gives only in the "meeting together" with other believers.'[11] Both the preacher and the viewer go through this experience. It is a psychological challenge to preach to empty pews with a picture of the members in mind. The emotions that go with the message will be fundamentally missed, and this will surely have impact on the import of the message on the viewers. There is a wide margin of difference in the emotions that accompany an already recorded corporate worship service when transmitted on social media or TV. Members also have that sense of disconnect viewing the online services, especially for those who were not used to the experience before the pandemic.

---

[11] Donald S. Whitney, *Spiritual Discipline for Christians* (Colorado Springs: NavPress, 1997), 92

Incomplete Elements of Public Worship on Social Media or TV

Virtual services on ECWA TV and other social media platforms focus on certain essential elements of worship in ECWA. Some of the essential features of corporate worship ignored are offering and Holy Communion. Many churches during the COVID-19 lockdown saw a hug dip in giving. Why? Most people feel like they are paying for a service. Now that they are not attending church physically, they feel no need to pay for the service. Are church services commodities? What happens to the church which solely depends on tithes and offerings? How will pastors and church staff get paid? What needs to change? The experience varies. Those churches where online giving has been in practice before the COVID-19 lockdown, have some of their members send in their offering electronically. And this was the case with most churches within the ECWA local church network.

Another important aspect in this regards was that of the Holy Communion. In ECWA, members were without communion until the coronavirus lockdown ban was lifted. In Pentecostal churches, however, there were circulars sent to members on how to prepare the elements at home and wait for a blessing over the screen. This has affected the finances of the church and the quality of believers' spirituality. Believers have access to a wide range of virtual church services through social media. This could be to their advantage and disadvantage. Some advantages include ecumenism, the fostering of unity in the body of Christ, and the opportunity to reach many with the gospel. However, believers' access to all sorts of preaching, teaching and practices online also have the tendency of endangering their spiritual lives. This development has the potential of swaying the loyalty of some to ECWA, as well as increasing their faith in Jesus Christ. This is not impossible for Christians who are young in faith.

CHAPTER SEVEN
EVANGELICAL RESPONSE TO CORONAVIRUS LOCKDOWN: THE CASE OF ECWA

Like a thief in the night, the coronavirus pandemic caught everybody unawares. No one saw it coming. Even prophets who claimed to have foreseen it were not specific, and as such, they lacked the boldness to warn or prepare the world beforehand. They only spoke out in retrospect after the pandemic had almost drowned the low and the high of our contemporary world. The swift and devastating impact of the pandemic left everyone dumbfounded for some while. Who would ever have imagined that an outbreak that broke out in the Wuhan city of mainland China would have touched the length and breadth of the world in less than six months? A development that was first reported to WHO on December 31,

2019 was declared a pandemic and a public health emergency only a month later (30 January, 2020).

The church also entered a state of initial shock. This shock came along with confusion as to how best to respond, especially when the preventive and containment measures of social distancing, partial and total lockdown set in. World leaders, nations, governments, states, organizations and individuals responded differently. Who would know how best to respond to such a global emergency at the onset? The church was not an exception to the global hullaballoo. Leadership was required in order to determine what the next steps were. This leadership was needed at every level and strata of society. Owing to the high regard that Nigerians hold their religious leaders, more was expected of them at this stage. Our goal at this point, therefore, is to underscore the specific ways that ECWA responded to the coronavirus pandemic and its accompanying challenges.

Call to Patriotism, Unity and Love

The leadership of ECWA swung into action as soon as the federal government issued directives restricting social gathering and free human movement. Initial responses came from the leadership of the District Churches of the first three states affected by the lockdown – Lagos, Ogun and FCT. Almost immediately afterwards, the leadership of ECWA issued circulars encouraging all ECWA members to take precaution, stay safe and obey the directives of government and healthcare workers. Members were asked to display patriotism, love and unity. This became expedient after government barred all religious houses from meeting physically. Many churches and their leaders in Nigeria complied with this directive. Sadly, some church leaders were arrested for flouting the rule and for instructing their followers to do likewise.

ECWA leadership modelled biblical Christianity by mobilizing its members to be patriotic, loving and obedient to constituted authorities.[1] Considering the effect of coronavirus pandemic lockdown on the church, its decision to obey the government all the same was a hard one. But, as I had argued earlier, the directive issued by the government was for the good of all. The closure of churches even affected the year 2020 Easter Celebration. However, it was on record that some leaders mobilized their members to attend corporate worship in spite of the directives of government. Some religious leaders were even arrested, prosecuted and jailed for violating government bans on public gathering. This did not give the church a good image, especially among unbelievers to whom we are called to model Christ.

The Bible enjoins Christians to be obedient and submissive to the authorities and be involved in the development of their society (Matthew 22:21; Romans 13:1–17). However, according to Samuel Kunhiyop, there were instances in the New Testament that the church acted against the state (Acts 5:29). There were even cases when political and religious leaders were described with derogatory names to indicate their hostility and hate for the church (Luke 13:32 and Revelation 13).[2] But those instances were recorded to show

---

[1] Stephen Baba Panya, 'Updates on COVID-19 Pandemic by the ECWA President' in *ECWA eCommunicator*: https://www.ecwausa.com/2020/04/17/updates-on-covid-19-pandemic-by-the-ecwa-president-17-april-2020/ Posted on April 17, 2020, Accessed on April 28, 2020. See also Peter Amine, 'COVID-19: ECWA Declares 3-Day Fasting and Prayer for God's Intervention' in *NNN*: https://nnn.com.ng/covid-19-ecwa-decalares-3-day-fasting-prayers-for-gods-intervention/ Posted on March 31, 2020, Accessed on April 10, 2020.

[2] Samuel Waje Kunhiyop, *African Christian Ethics* (Nairobi: World Alive Publishers, 2008), 91.

the disposition of the state, political and religious leaders towards the church. Those Scriptures should not be used as the basis for disobeying constituted authorities. We must bear in mind that the early church was a missionary church in transition within a hostile context, and so, some of their experiences may not be applied to the successive church as it comes of age. In Matthew 22:21, Jesus stresses our responsibility as Christians to God and government, and he enjoined us not to default in both. In Romans 13, the Bible stresses in verse one: *'Let everyone be subject to the governing authorities, for there is no authority except that which God has established. The authorities that exist have been established by God'* (NIV). Apostle Peter also emphasised the importance of this in 2 Peter 2:13-17.

Consequently, if all constituted authorities come from God, then to disobey them and the institutions they stand for is tantamount to disobeying God. Considering the African context, oftentimes it is hard to admit that God is involved in the emergence of some political and religious leaders. This position is precipitated by the evil that some of these leaders perpetuate while in office. But the Bible enjoins us to obey, all the same. We were even required to pray for them (Jeremiah 29:7 and 1 Timothy 2:1-2). And even when the actions of our leaders present them to us as our enemies, the Bible teaches Christians to *'love ... and to pray for our enemies'* (Matthew 5: 43-47, NIV). Our true identity in Christ is made obvious to the dying world when we submit to constituted authorities, love and prayer for those who act in and against our interests amongst our leaders. That is Evangelical Christianity.

Call to Repentance, Hope and Prayer for Revival

The social, political and religious context of Nigeria was already in a precarious state, even before the coronavirus outbreak. The wanton destruction of human lives and properties by the *Boko Haram* religious extremists had reached a scary state. The Nigerian government seemed to have exhausted all ideas in confronting this menace. Cases of banditry, kidnapping, cattle rustling, extrajudicial killings, general insecurity, political impunity and corruption were growing at an alarming rate. What shall we say of lack of basic social amenities? Of unemployment? And of corruption? Many citizens had entered a state of fatalism, apathy and lethargy. Unfortunately, religious institutions that should be the conscience of the society had also failed the public on many instances. The Nigerian social context was already tense before coronavirus. The coming of COVID-19 served to aggravate the tension and further expose the delicate situation.

Prayer seemed to be the last and only hope of the common man. Prayer could not have been the only antidote, but the efficacy of its power in helping to resolve our already complicated situation cannot be over-emphasised. The leadership of ECWA took the opportunity to invite its members and the entire Christian community of Nigeria to go back to prayer and put their hope in Christ. Christians were urged to repent and seek God's face for revival. Before this time, there was already a growing hostility against prayer. This is was more pronounced in social media. Some Nigerians were beginning to critique the mindset of extreme spiritualization as the predominant tool for interpreting the world around them. This critique sees this mindset as the bane behind Nigeria's lack of development in that it weakens religious adherents from taking responsibility for their actions. Consequently, there is a growing revival dissension against religion. An increasing number of Nigerians consider religion as one of the enemies of development.

Interestingly, the outbreak of coronavirus brought some sobriety and has caused many to consider repairing their relationships with

God. It is true that prayer should complement and not replace human responsibility. It is also true that, as a people, we have woefully failed in our individual and collective responsibilities to our nation. We have thrown away our responsibility, largely in the name of religiosity. Even that *religiosity* is, to a large extent, non-compliant with divine standards and the *tenets* of our *faiths*. That is why they're mere religiosities.

Nevertheless these are not enough excuses to trivialize the power of prayer and our dependence in God. God has, in countless ways, shown his sovereignty in the midst of our individual and collective capabilities and fragility–COVID-19 is just one additional way. The Bible says in Proverbs 21:31 that, *'The horse is made ready for the day of battle, but victory rests with the LORD'* (NIV). By mobilizing its members to invest more time in prayer during the challenging COVID-19 lockdown, ECWA has proven it believes in prayer and its power to bring a season of refreshment upon our land. This is one of the many ways ECWA is contributing to the development of our society and is also an indication that there are still individuals, organizations and religious institutions doing the same.

Call to Personal Piety and Family Revival

Evangelical Christianity promotes individual commitment to spiritual growth. While it is true the corporate worship occupies a strategic place in the spiritual growth of a Christian, it must be preceded by a personal commitment to Christ. The commitment is a lifelong journey. A Christian should be self-directed in the commitment to grow spiritually. The emphasis on taking initiatives for individual spiritual growth starts at the entry point of the Christian faith. The Bible in John 3:16 states: *'For God so loved the* world that he gave his one and only Son, that whoever believes in him shall not perish but have eternal life' (NIV). The phrase 'whoever' indicates that the appropriation of the salvation package of God should be individually. After the salvation package of God has been appropriated, it is the believer's duty to make a lifelong personal commitment to a daily work with Christ.

Jesus stresses the importance of this in Luke 9:23, 'Then he said to them all: *"Whoever wants to be my disciple must deny themselves and take up their cross daily and follow me'* (NIV). This indicates a personal daily walk with Christ. This is known as discipleship, and its importance to the believer's spiritual growth is scattered all through the Bible. The explanation of Luke 9:23 as provided by Paul John Isaak is helpful for our understanding here. According to him:

> The followers of Jesus are summoned to *take up their cross* day after day. As used by Jesus, taking up one's cross daily means that discipleship is a most painful task because it is a self-giving and self-forgetting, like dragging a cross for one's own execution. Taking up the cross means that the Christian life is a dying life to self, much like Paul does when he says, 'I die every day' (1 Corinthians 15:31, ICB).[3]

The reflection above insinuates that Jesus invited his followers to follow his own example of self-sacrifice and submission to the will of his Father (Philippians 2:3-11). Jesus modelled to his followers the virtues of love, sacrifice, humility, discipline, dedication and loyalty. These and many others are what discipleship entails. Believers are invited on an individual basis to follow the example of Jesus as a

---

[3] Paul John Isaak, 'Luke' in *Africa Bible Commentary*, Tokunboh Adeyemo, ed., (Nairobi: WordAlive Publishers, 2006), 1222.

student or an apprentice follows a master. However, Tokunboh Adeyemo opines that, 'Being a disciple involves more than just being s student. It implies a personal attachment to a particular person who shapes the disciple's whole life.'[4] The gist here is the word *attachment*.

To be attached to someone is be fond of him or her. To be fond of someone is to be loving, caring, obedient, loyal and committed to the individual, even against all odds. Attachment can be both physical and spiritual. Physical attachment may be challenged by geography, but this is not so with spiritual attachment. Spiritual attachment is an intimate experience that cannot be challenged by geography, time or other forms of physical barriers. This truth is established in John 4:24 as the Bible states that, *'God is spirit, and his worshippers must worship in Spirit and in truth'* (NIV). This kind of worship cannot be limited by time and location. It is an informal kind of worship and attachment. It is an attachment that connects the spirit of man to that of God. It is an inseparable bond because it is a connection between the Spirit of God and the spirit of man. The inseparability of this connection is what Paul refers to in Romans 8:35-39:

> Who shall separate us from the love of Christ? Shall trouble or hardship or persecution or famine or nakedness or danger or sword? As it is written: "For your sake we face death all day long; we are considered as sheep to be slaughtered." No, in all these things we are more than conquerors through him who loved us. For I am convinced that neither death nor life, neither angels nor demons, neither the present nor the future, nor any powers, neither height nor depth, nor anything else in all creation,

---

[4] Tokunboh Adeyemo, 'Discipleship' *Africa Bible Commentary*, Tokunboh Adeyemo, ed., (Nairobi: WordAlive Publishers, 2006), 1223.

will be able to separate us from the love of God that is in Christ Jesus our Lord (NIV).

The inseparability of the bond is not based on the power of man but on the love of Christ. This is the kind of attachment that discipleship with Christ entails. Christ is indispensable to the believer. Someone is said to be indispensable when certain things could not be done without this person. Through discipleship, a believer has agreed to a life of daily commitment with Christ. And so, for the disciple, a daily walk with Christ is indispensable. This is the invitation that Christ gives in Matthew 11: 28-30. '*Come to me, all you who are weary and burdened, and I will give you rest. Take my yoke upon you and learn from me, for I am gentle and humble in heart, and you will find rest for your souls. For my yoke is easy and my burden is light*' (NIV).

Faithful disciples, Adeyemo stresses, 'are characterized by qualities such as abiding in Jesus's word, steadfast faith in him, loyalty to him, love for one another, walking in the light, bearing fruit and humble service to one another (John 8:31–36; 13:34–35).'[5] This kind of Christianity is unusual in Nigerian society today. There is little wonder why the impact of Christianity on the moral fabric of Nigerian society is so minimal today. Ironically, Nigeria has one of the largest concentrations of *Christians* in the world today, and yet, it is acclaimed as one of the most corrupt nations in the modern world. Where is the impact of Christianity in the Nigerian public square? The leadership of ECWA responded to the coronavirus lockdown by challenging its members to go back to biblical Christianity. The window of *opportunity* created by the lockdown is timeless and should be seized by Christians to invest in their personal attachments to Christ. This can be attained by living a life of personal and daily

---

[5] Tokunboh Adeyemo, 'Discipleship', 1223.

commitment to the Word of God, meditation, prayer, holy living, obedience to the Word of God and several other spiritual discipline too numerous to exhaust here. The goal of this is to grow in faith and become more like Christ.

With the help of the Holy Spirit, the journey of maturation in Christ is possible, even in times when there are no opportunities to be physically involved in corporate worship. This lack of opportunity may be occasioned by several factors. One such factor is the one that this book is addressing – Coronavirus lockdown. Others could be government policies and Christian persecution. Of course, there nations in our contemporary world where Christians could not undertake corporate worship due to government policy and persecution.

The early church readily comes to mind when it comes to the problem of persecution and the challenges that it posed to corporate worship. We see examples of such persecutions in Acts 7:54–60 and Acts 8:1–3. This was what led to the dispersion of early Christians throughout Judea and Samaria. Going forward, the Jerusalem church continued and spread beyond the shores of Jerusalem as House churches. Examples are in Acts 2:46; 5:42; 8:3; 10:22; 12:12; 16:32,40; 18:7; 20:20; Romans 16:5; 1 Corinthians 16:19; Colossians 4:15 and Philemon. Although this initiative never stopped the Christians from being persecuted (Acts 8:1), it is one of the means that God used to expand the church to where it is today. Paul, who later converted to Christianity, and many other leaders of the church went through some form of lockdown that lasted for short and longer periods of time. But the results observed in their lives indicate that they continued in their attachment with Christ, even to the very end of their lives. For instance, four out of the thirteen books of the New Testament, excluding Hebrews, were written in prison (Acts 28:16; 28:30, 31 and Philippians 4:22). The Prison Epistles are Ephesians,

Philippians, Colossians and Philemon. Three of these churches were the churches he founded on his second missionary journey (Acts 20:1-3). The principles taught in these book are invaluable for Christians of all generations. The revelation of events of the end of times was revealed to John while in isolation on the Island of Patmos (Revelation 1:9).

Apart from the government and persecution induced lockdown of confinement, self-isolation for the purpose of communing with God was a practice that was commonly modelled by Jesus (Matthew 14:23; 26:36,39,42,44; Mark 1:35; 6:46; 14:32, 35; Luke 5:16; 6:12; 9:18). Agreed, Jesus's withdrawal from the public in the scripture cited earlier was not imposed but self-motivated. This principle promotes occasional self-withdrawal for the purpose of self-evaluation and communion with God as a route to spiritual maturation. The COVID-19 lockdown can serve as an opportunity for this.

But beyond this, ECWA also instructed family heads to take advantage of the time to invest in devotion with their family members. This challenge was particularly thrown at fathers and husbands to provide spiritual leadership to families as the head of their homes. This was precipitated by the biblical injunction given in Ephesians 5:23; 25-33; 6:4. It is one of the fundamental requirements for taking up positions of leadership in the church (1Timothy 3:4-5). Abraham, Joshua and Job are examples of men who pleased God in the management of their homes (Genesis 18:19; Joshua 24:15; Job 1:5). The ramifications of nurturing our families in the way of the Lord goes beyond the church; you and I will agree that it has huge implications on society. ECWA used the opportunity of the lockdown to mobilize family leaders to show an example in this regard.

Call to Salvation and Readiness for the Second Coming of Christ

Some of the most frequently preached messages on ECWA TV and its social media platform during the period of the lockdown were those of salvation and the Second Coming of Christ. As earlier established, the media provides preachers and Bible teachers the opportunity to reach a vast range of audience within a relatively short period. The opportunity of the social media platform was also being seized to reach its members and present the message of salvation to unbelievers who may come in contact with such messages. Since the ban on free movement of humans during this time was a barrier to physical meetings, the ministry of the Media Department of ECWA came in handy. Though highly capital intensive, the establishment of Radio ELWA and ECWA TV served to achieve this purpose. This period provided a window of opportunity for personal and lifestyle evangelism, particularly to family members who are unsaved.

In his Easter 2020 message, ECWA President, Rev Stephen Panya Baba said, 'While there is no doubt that the coronavirus pandemic is a sign of the beginning of the end times and the very terrible times of great tribulation ahead, the good news of great joy is that [this] tribulation period will be proceeded by a time of great revival of [the] harvest of souls.'[6] Believers were admonished to view coronavirus as one of the signs of the end of time and should get ready for the coming revival and Second Coming of Christ. Only God can determine the impact of all these on believers and unbelievers alike.

---

[6] Stephen Panyan Baba, 'ECWA President's Easter 2020 Speech' in https://youtu.be/DGtHY4nqBnw/ Accessed on April 18, 2020.

Christ Is the Answer

In a context where emphasis on material wealth is oftentimes more pronounced than the name, person and ministry of Jesus, the need to emphasize the centrality of Jesus to the biblical message is both urgent and crucial. This should be the primary mission of Evangelical Christianity. This is the fact but the reality is sometimes different. In narration of the impact of prosperity gospel on African church and society, Femi Adeleye laments that:

> We face a major crisis today. A number of people have told me how they go to church longing to encounter Jesus, and how disappointed they have been that Jesus has often been marginalized both by the "men of God" and everything else that transpires in church. Jesus and the proclamation of the gospel keep being squeezed into oblivion by "more important matter" – blessing the minister, celebrating a birthday, commemorating a car or building and multiple appeals for funds.[7]

While giving thanks to God in the presence of his people for his goodness towards us is in itself not wrong, the motive behind such celebrations remains the issue. Are we celebrating to glorify *the God of man* or to boost the ego of the *man of God*? It is unfortunate that many Christians today are living below the biblical standard, thereby hindering unbelievers from seeing Jesus. Prosperity gospel has made our faith in Christ worrisomely shallow. According to Tozer:

---

[7] Femi Adeleye, *Preacher of a Different Gospel* (Nairobi: HippoBooks, 2011), 45.

> Evangelical Christianity ... is now tragically below the New Testament Standard. Worldliness is an acceptable part of our way of life. Our religious mood is social instead of spiritual. We have lost the art of worship. We are not practicing saints. Our models are successful businessmen, celebrated athletes and the worldly personalities. We carry out religious activities after the model of the modern advertiser... Our literature is shallow and scarcely anyone appears to care.[8]

Success is now being judged by the type of car one rides, the number of cars one possesses, the type of house one stays and the kinds of clothing we wear. Being materially poor is seen as an effect of sin. Many Christians in our times are lacking genuine biblical Christianity because they have a wrong concept of God and that of themselves. The warning of Tozer is succinct here when he warns: 'We must have a better kind of Christianity soon or within another half century or we may have no true Christianity at all. Increased number of demi-Christians is not enough. We must have reformation.'[9] Tozer's pronouncement is truer now than when it was first made. The unquenchable want of money by some of our political leaders cannot be totally divorced from this misleading teaching being popularized by some preachers in Nigeria. The truth is, if all who claimed to be Christians were genuine, our nation would have been better for it. Sadly, some spiritual leaders who are supposed to lead by example are themselves guilty of the same sin.

ECWA emphasized the centrality of Jesus to the whole of

---

[8] A.W. Tozer, 'The First Obligation of the Church,' *Herald of His Coming*, (January 2002), 4.
[9] Ibid.

life. Jesus is the answer to all of human's questions. In the ECWA President's Easter 2020 Speech, Reverend Stephen Baba, in a speech of 1140 words, mentioned *Jesus* twenty-four times, *Christ* thirteen times, *Lord* thirteen times and Saviour six times. Thus the name and title of Jesus was mentioned fifty-six times which amounted to over 20% of the speech.[10] Using the tool of content analysis[11], we can conclude that Jesus was the focus of the message. How is mentioning the name of Jesus a number times the answer to all human questions? What more can one expect in an Easter message given by a denominational head? Let us turn our lenses to Baba's perspectives on the coronavirus and Jesus. First, his message focused on Jesus as the Saviour of humankind, and so, people should look only to Jesus for salvation and deliverance. Second, he presented Jesus as the true healer, and so, believers should look only to him for personal and global healing against all forms of diseases, specifically

---

[10] Stephen Panya Baba, 'ECWA President's Easter 2020 Speech' in *Truth and Honour* https://ama924.wordpress.com/2020/04/06/ecwa-presidents-easter-2020-speech/?fbclid=IwAR2EiComCAoArz0uBFYoc9Qok_5iq0RN7dM3Sv2yjrtqnsaAN6-xRFg0wcY/ Posted on April 6, 2020.

[11] According to Kondracki and others, 'content analysis is used to develop objective inferences about a subject of interest in any type of media text. The process of content analysis consists of coding raw message such as textual material, visual images or illustrations, according to a classification scheme. The coding process is essentially one of organizing media content in a manner that allows for easy identification, indexing, or retrieval of content relevant to research questions.' Content components may comprise words, themes, phrase, theories, topics, concepts or characteristics. The content components are otherwise known in literature as units of data analysis. Content analysis enabled me to draw thematic inferences on the representation in the ECWA President's Easter 2020 Speech (See Nancy L. Kondracki, et al., 'Content Analysis: Review of Methods and Their Applications in Nutrition Education,' *Journal of Nutrition Education and Behavior,* Vol. 34 (2002), 224; and Naomi Brock, 'Representations of Nigerian Women in Nollywood Films,' MA Thesis: Howard University, Washington (Dec., 2009), 13).

COVID-19. Third, he presented Jesus as the giver of hope and that he could offer true hope to all who put their hopes in him.[12] The word of Femi Adeleye is apt for our conclusion here: 'Jesus must be restored to his rightful position in the church he owns.'[13] ECWA has, through his message to its members during the coronavirus lockdown, reminded the global church of its primary mission. And is this not the crux of Evangelical Christianity?

---

[12] Stephen Panya Baba, 'ECWA President's Easter 2020 Speech' in *Truth and Honour*.

[13] Femi Adeleye, 46.

CHAPTER EIGHT
INSIGHTS FOR THE FUTURE OF ECWA

In the previous chapters, we looked at the essential elements of corporate worship in ECWA. We examined the effects and response of ECWA to the coronavirus lockdown. But does ECWA have the capacity to navigate through the coronavirus lockdown challenges? How has ECWA contributed to the development of Nigeria before the COVID-19 pandemic? Does ECWA need any skills in order to remain relevant and focused on its vision and mission in the post-coronavirus world? This chapter concerns itself with providing answers to these questions.

ECWA History in a Glance

You will notice that this study has, until now, been silent on the history of the Evangelical Church Winning All. This is because narratives on the origin and history of the denomination are in the public domain for any interested individuals to access. Be that as it may, a summative review of ECWA history is now necessary in order to properly situate this chapter.

The missionary process that gave birth to ECWA came from the Holy Spirit through the vision and efforts of Margaret Gowans, Walter Gowans, Thomas Kent and Rowland Bingham. Towards the close of the nineteenth century, the Lord placed a burden to pray for the harvest of unsaved people in Africa on the heart of Mrs. Margaret Gowans, a native Scot who migrated from Scotland with her family to Toronto, Canada. Little did she know that the Lord would later answer her prayers by calling her son, Walter Gowans, and two other young men to labour on the ripe field of Africa. Walter Gowans was a Scottish-Canadian, Thomas Kent was an American and Rowland Bingham was an English Canadian. Bingham, like the Gowans, also migrated from England to Canada in the year 1889. These three young men had affiliations with three different Evangelical denominations. Walter Gowans was of the Presbyterian Church, Thomas Kent was of the Baptist Church and Rowland Bingham was of the Salvation Army. These three made their first ecumenical missionary effort to the shores of Nigeria in the year 1893. In 1893, Walter was twenty-three years of age, while Thomas and Rowland were twenty-five and twenty-one years of age, respectively. This ecumenical spirit was compatible with the mission practice in Africa in the nineteenth century. Missionary societies did many things in common, irrespective of denominational differences.[1]

---

[1] Ian Fleck, *Bringing Christianity to Nigeria: The Origin and Work of Protestant Missions* (Bukuru: Africa Christian Textbooks, 2013), 25.

EVANGELICAL RESPONSE TO THE CORONAVIRUS LOCKDOWN

The first missionary attempts of Walter Gowans, Thomas Kent and Rowland Bingham in Nigeria failed, owing to a number of factors. First was the disturbing news about the death of missionaries who had travelled to *Sudan* before them. An unfortunate statement was credited to Byrau Roe, a superintendent of the Wesleyan Mission in Lagos who said to the young missionaries that 'You will never see Sudan; your children will never see Sudan – your grandchildren may.' No one knows exactly why Roe uttered such devastating comment. Could it have been based on his personal experiences or those of other missionaries in the region? Or could it have been because the three missionaries were young and he thought they are not mature enough to survive the struggles of the African mission fields? We are not privy to his reasons. We can only expect that his discouraging words sank deep into the minds of these missionaries. Rough terrain, unfavorable weather condition and ill health are some of the known factors that stood in the way of the first effort of Walter, Thomas and Bingham. These efforts were under a mission agency named Sudan Interior Mission. According to E.A Adeyemi, 'The name Sudan Interior Mission (SIM) was adopted by pioneers of a Christian Mission whose sole objective was to open the Sudan, the land of the blacks from the West to the East of Africa between the equator and Sahara desert, to the Gospel . . . of Christ."[2]

Even though the name of the mission went through several changes within a short period of time, one is sure of the fact that the purpose of the mission stands still. According to Adeyemi, 'reasons for these frequent changes in name within seven years are not clear. The aim, however, remained unchanged at any time; the sixty million lives

---

[2] E. A. Adeyemi, *From Seven to Seven Thousand: The Story of the Birth and Growth of SIM/ECWA Church in Ilorin* (Ilorin: Okinbaloye Commercial Press, 1995), 11.

in the "dark Sudan" must be reached for Christ.'³ The Sudan Interior Mission existed in this name for several years under the leadership of Walter Gowans, Thomas Kent and Rowland Bingham. It took several years for the work to come to the limelight but it eventually came. Several attempts were made before it finally yielded fruits. To be precise, the first and second attempts spanned between 1893 and 1900 and were full of discouragements strong enough to kill the vision.

Just like the old biblical Prophet in 1 Kings 13:11-19, the discouraging declaration of Byrau Roe seemed to be a discouraging prophetic declaration that was permitted by God to come to pass in the lives of two out of the three missionaries. Walter Gowans and Thomas Kent later died while on the mission. The death of these two pioneer leaders caused a setback. On the 17th or 18th of November 1894, Walter Gowans (The initiator and leader of the group) died at Garku, a little town near Zaria. Thomas Kent also died of malaria at Bida, Niger State, on December 8, 1894.⁴ Bingham's illness during his second attempt did not help the matter, either, but he refused to let go of the vision.

The death of the two leaders compelled Rowland Bingham to go back to his country, Canada, for better prepare. Although the past experience was not a sweet one for Bingham, he decided not to leave the prospect unaccomplished after several years of labour. Perhaps, Bingham thought the vision which his two associates had laboured and sacrificed their lives for must not be aborted unaccomplished. The good news, however, is that the third attempt, when Rowland Bingham returned to Africa, brought a watershed to SIM. Against all odds, and through the grace of God, the third attempt paid off with the establishment of the first mission station in Patigi. The years that followed, particularly from 1901 to 1914, saw the rapid expansion of

---

³ Ibid.,
⁴ D. I. Olatayo, *ECWA: The Root, Birth and Growth*, 3.

SIM. This was the genesis of the expansion of SIM in Nigeria and Africa as a whole. The next forty years saw a phenomenal growth of SIM in Nigeria. Its initial expansion succeeded immensely in the northern part of the country.

As the independent process began, the leadership of SIM thought it necessary to hand over the mission to indigenous leaders. In 1954, all converts in the local churches planted by SIM in Nigeria came together and formed an indigenous denomination under the name the Evangelical Churches of West Africa. They adopted a form of church government and registered the organization with the Government of Nigeria as a religious body on 11 June 1956 and as an approved Voluntary Agency in June 1958. This is the nucleus of what is now the Evangelical Church Winning All. The need to bear a name that captured the spread of the denomination beyond the shores of Nigeria and West Africa to other parts of world informed the change from the Evangelical Church of West Africa to the Evangelical Church Winning All in 2011.

ECWA is one of the foremost evangelical denominations in Africa. It has over 6000 congregations and 10 million members. ECWA has its international headquarters in Jos in Plateau State of Nigeria but has members in some western and Eastern African countries, as well as in the United Kingdom and the United States of America. ECWA has the largest missionary organization in Africa and one of the most established missionary bodies in the contemporary world church. The Nigerian church has been adjudged the third largest national evangelical church in the world. ECWA occupies a front seat in the evaluation. The Evangelical Missionary Society (EMS) of ECWA has about 2000 missionaries serving in Nigeria and abroad. ECWA now has three major seminaries, eight Bible schools, fifteen theological training institutes, over 110 health clinics, a major pharmaceutical outfit with a school of nursing and midwifery, several primary and post-primary schools, Radio ELWA, ECWA TV and ECWA Productions Limited, the printing and literature arm of the denomination.

Additionally, ECWA owns a microfinance bank named after Walter Gowans, a network of guest houses and Bingham University. Bingham University was named after Rowland Bingham, and its college of medicine is the first private university to be licensed by the government of Nigeria to run the degree. These investments are located in different parts of Nigeria, but the majority are in Jos, where the international headquarters of the church is situated. These are apart from the outreach and discipleship ministries of ECWA. ECWA occupies a front seat in the evaluation. Because of its emphasis on sound biblical teaching, evangelism and discipleship, ECWA is regarded as one of most revered Evangelical denominations in Nigeria. These developments could not have been possible without the help of the Holy Spirit and the efforts of the founding fathers and mothers. The hand of God on the mission was further confirmed when some relatives of Rowland Bingham visited Nigeria from Canada and worshipped at the Cathedral of Christ Church, Marina, Lagos in November 2017. This was the same location where Byrau Roe said to the young missionaries that, 'You will never see Sudan; your children will never see Sudan–your grandchildren may.' Retrospectively, one can vividly see the hand of God on ECWA as a mission. Let us shift our attention on the role of ECWA in the sociopolitical development of Nigeria.

ECWA and the Creation of Social Capital

African Christianity as a whole has been criticized for being apolitical. Scholars have argued for and against its role in the development of the African society. Though focused essentially on Pentecostal Christianity in Africa, Paul Gifford, through his several studies on African Christianity blames the minimal performance of African Christianity on misleading hermeneutical approach, misuse of media for self-promotion of pastors, over-reliance on the West, materialist culture and enchanted Christianity.[5] Other scholars have, however, argued otherwise. Notable among these scholars was Ogbu Kalu. He argued that the involvement of the African church to societal development should be examined against African epistemologies and cultural prisms. Without this, Kalu opines that our understanding of the role of the church in the societal development of Africa will be misplaced and misleading.[6]

Kalu argues that the role of the African church in sociopolitical issues cannot be understated. Its role in the fight against HIV/AIDS in South Africa is one of many examples. Kalu submits that Pentecostalism has given hope to Africans by attacking sin, which is responsible for the degradations that befall the human dignity as well as the prosperity of the society - 'rebuilding the individual'; by 'redeeming the land' from the power of darkness through power; by 'building a beloved community' of a tight 'ecumenical bonding'; through prayer for the government and political leaders – 'intercession as political praxis'; by vying for political offices where

---

[5] See Paul Gifford, *Christianity, Development and Modernity in Africa* (London: Hurst & Company, 2015), 1; and Christianity, *Politics and Public Life in Kenya* .London: Hurst & Co., 2009; Ghana's New Christianity. *Pentecostalism in a Globalising African Economy.* London: Hurst & Company, 2004; *African Christianity: Its Public Role.* C Hurst & Co. London: 1998.

[6] Ogbu Kalu, 'Yabbing the Pentecostals: Paul Gifford's Image of Ghana's New Christianity,' African *Pentecostalism: Global Discourses, Migrations and Exchange and Connects,* Wilhelmina J. Kalu, Nimi Wariboko, and Toyin Fabola, eds., (Trenton, NJ: Africa World Press, Inc., 2010), 149-162. See also Ogbu Kalu, *African Pentecostalism: An Introduction,* 108-110.

necessary.[7] He adds that African Pentecostalism gives hope by rebuilding the individual, thus bestowing them the power to be truly human; by a predominantly covert form of social activism, attacking socio-political and moral structures; through an increasing assertion for the rule of saints and the politics of engagement and building the new Israel by empowering communities to participate in the foretaste of God's reign.

It thus breaks the dichotomy between the various categories –individual and society, private and public – using the resource of the gospel to weave a multifaceted and holistic response to the human predicament in the African ecosystem.[8] He continues saying 'the achievement of Pentecostals lies in their innovative responses to the challenges embedded in the African map of the universe.'[9] He concludes that the Church should not lose the balance in a *pluralistic world* as a result of involvement in politics.[10] While the Kalu's seems convincing, that of Gifford serves as a warning for the church that it may not fail in its primary duty to God and the people. Our reason for the views above is to briefly examine the contribution of ECWA to Nigeria's development, even before the COVID-19 outbreak. This would be viewed against its creation of social capital.

The term *social capital* is used in several different ways in fields like political science, economics, sociology and anthropology. According to Luka Deng, 'Social Capital has gained considerable appeal in recent years and has dominated debates in both the theoretical and applied science literature, where it is frequently seen as crucial to promoting economic growth and fostering good governance. Although this is a relatively new concept to economists,

---

[7] Ogbu Kalu, *African Pentecostalism: An Introduction*, 207-223.
[8] Ibid.
[9] Ibid., 186.
[10] Ibid., 197.

anthropologists have long recognized the crucial role played by social capital in the development of human societies.'[11] In all cases, the use of this concept boils down to the idea that people create connections with each other, and these connections are used in a variety of ways. Thus, social capital is the network of relationships between individuals, groups and entities. Studying social capital can be a way to learn about how a society functions.[12]

There's much debate over the various forms that social capital takes, but one fairly straightforward approach divides it into three main categories: *Bonds* which are links to people based on a sense of common identity (i.e., people like us) – such as family, close friends and people who share our culture or ethnicity; *Bridges* such as links that stretch beyond a shared sense of identity, for example to distant friends, colleagues and associates; and *Linkages*, which are links to people or groups further up or lower down the social ladder.[13]

The term *social capital*, according to Robert Putnam and Kristin Goss, 'is a term coined in 1916 by L. Judson Hanifan, a young progressive educator and social reformer who was a native of West Virginia in the United States of America.'[14] Hanifan trained in some

---

[11] Luka Biong Deng, 'Social capital and civil war: The Dinka communities in Sudan's civil war,' *The Journal of the Royal African Society*, Volume 109, Number 435 (April, 2010), 232.

[12] 'What is social capital?' in http://www.wisegeek.com/what-is-social-capital.htm (culled on Wednesday December 1, 2010).

[13] 'What is social capital?' in Organization for Economic Co-operation and Development (OECD) Insight: http://www.oecd.org/dataoecd/36/6/37966934.pdf (culled on Wednesday December 1, 2010), 2. See also Luka Biong Deng, 'Social Capital and Civil War: The Dinka Communities in Sudan's Civil War' *African Affairs: The Journal of the Royal African Society*, Volume 109, No. 435 (April, 2009), 232.

[14] Robert D. Putnam and Kristin A Goss, 'Introduction' in *Democracies in a Flux: The Evolution of Social Capital in Contemporary Society*, ed. Robert D. Putnam (Oxford: Oxford Press, 2002), 4.

of the best universities in America, and after the completion of his training, he returned to his state, West Virginia, as a rural school teacher.[15] Putnam and Goss described the state of West Virginia during those times as an *impoverished state*.[16] In their portrait, 'Hanifan, throughout his years of teaching and observations, soon discovered that the grave social, economic and political problems of the communities in which he worked could be solved only by strengthening the network of solidarity among their citizens.'[17] Hanifan 'observed that older customs of rural neighborliness and civic engagement, such as debating societies, barn raisings and apple cuttings had fallen to disuse, and gradually, these customs became almost wholly abandoned, the people becoming less neighborly. As a result, community social life gave way to family isolation and community stagnation.'[18] Quoting directly from Hanifan, Putnam and Goss went on to define the term *social capital* as follows:

> In the use of the phrase social capital I make no reference to the usual acceptation of the term capital, except in figurative sense. I do not refer to real estate, or to personal property or to cold cash but rather to that in life which tends to make these tangible substances count for most in the daily lives of the people, namely good will, fellowship, mutual sympathy and social intercourse among individuals and families who make up a society unit . . . The individual is helpless socially, if left to himself . . . If he comes into contact with his neighbor, and they

---

[15] Ibid.
[16] Ibid.
[17] Ibid.
[18] Putnam and Goss, *Democracies in Flux*, 4.

with other neighbors, there will be an accumulation of social capital, which may immediately satisfy his social needs and which may bear a social potentiality sufficient to the substantial improvement of the living condition in the whole community.[19]

Thus social capital has benefits to the individual as well as to the public, and they include a low rate of crime in neighborhoods and social connectedness amongst the residents.[20] 'In many instances of social capital, some of the benefits go to bystanders, while some of the benefits serve the immediate interest of the person making the investment. For example, local civic clubs mobilize local energies to build a playground or a hospital at the same time that they provide members with friendship and business connections that pay off personally.'[21] Above all,

the community as a whole will benefit by the cooperation of all its parts, while the individual will find in his associations the advantages of the help, the sympathy, and the fellowship of his neighbors... When the people of a given community have become acquainted with one another and have formed the habit of coming together occasionally for entertainment, social intercourse, and a personal enjoyment... then by skillful leadership this social capital can easily be directed towards the general improvement of the community well-being.[22]

---

[19] Ibid.
[20] Ibid., 7.
[21] Ibid.
[22] Ibid., 4-5.

According to Claus Offe and Susanne Fuchs, 'religious orientation and strength of religious commitment are hypothesized to be positively correlated with social capital. Churches and other religious organizations act as catalysts of associational activity. For instance, by providing meeting rooms for environment groups, they foster the development of cooperative skills and enhance the awareness of social problems.' [23] Offe and Fuchs submit that 'religious commitment in general is a very strong predictor for membership in social service associations in Germany; and this is not unconnected with the Christian theology that puts emphasis upon the duty to serve fellow human beings.'[24] Following this backdrop, I submit that ECWA has since its inception been involved in the development of Nigeria through the Creation of social capital.

The denomination has been doing this in the society by mobilizing it adherents to be involved in democratization, as well providing infrastructures for meetings. ECWA, through its numerous spiritual activities, equips its members towards increasing morality. Additionally, the contributions of ECWA in the educational, health and rurally developed sections of Nigeria exist to serve the same purpose. What about economic development? ECWA has done considerably well in the areas of job creation and the sponsoring of several poverty alleviation initiatives. These have been achieved without the financial support of the government of Nigeria. However, the initial investments of ECWA in its education and health outreaches were largely funded through the effort of SIM from the West. But since the indigenization of the church in 1954, ECWA projects have been largely funded locally through proceeds from offerings, tithes, special fundraising, freewill donations, dues and by grant or with gifts.

---

[23] Offe and Fuchs, 208.
[24] Ibid.

Does ECWA Need Any Improvement?

Before this point, ECWA has been portrayed as a perfect human organization. There is no such organization, not even the church. Our world has been classified into two, the pre-coronavirus era and the post-coronavirus era. In the post-coronavirus era, everything is changing about how we live, think, work, study, travel, worship and do business and relate to one another. Our dispositions to that change will determine what the post-coronavirus world will look like for us. Rigidity will be a great undoing for many in the days to come. We all have to prepare to learn, unlearn and relearn new skills in order to survive this pandemic and after. The church in Africa, and indeed ECWA, is not immune to the changes taking place. If the church in Africa and beyond is to survive and be of impact, then it must be like the men of Issachar, '... *who understood the times and knew what Israel should do* . . .' (1 Chronicles 12:32, NIV). We must understand and accept that times have changed. Our concern here is to underscore the areas where ECWA needs improvement in its responses to the effects of the coronavirus lockdown on corporate worship. What are their implications and the way forward for the future of the denomination? In our study of this phenomenon, we noticed two broad areas needing improvement.

Media and ICT: Implication for Youth Migration and Emigration

As explained earlier and later, at the extrapolation stage of this book, ECWA has performed considerably well in the area of information and communications technology. The importance of Radio ELWA, ECWA TV and ECWA Production Limited reached a fresh notability during the coronavirus lockdown. It served to reach many of its members and a wide range of other people with the Word of God. But while the urban, rich church members have internet, Wi-Fi, laptops, smart TVs and smart phones, the rural, poor folks lack these. A more detailed discussion and recommendation are offered in the next chapter. So, it suffices that we highlight this at this juncture as one of the areas that ECWA needs improvement for the future. Another major area is the use of social media platforms such as Facebook, Telegram, WhatsApp, Twitter, YouTube, Instagram, Zoom, Telegraph, Skype and the like. Prominent among them for the transmission of the gospel are Facebook, YouTube, WhatsApp, Instagram, Skype and Zoom. This is due to their video and interactive components.

Many Pentecostal-Charismatic denominations have invested because they were accustomed to the opportunities that lie in social media. Therefore, it was not difficult for them to maximize it during the lockdown as an alternative platform to worship, reaching their members and non-members alike. Some local ECWA churches tried, but several other local churches of the denomination were edged out by this challenge. The qualities of, and in some cases, the contents of productions were below standard when compared to the variety of bouquets on offer by other denominations. So, our members were left with the temptation to choose between *the good, the bad* and *the ugly*. Only God can determine how many members ECWA has lost to this temptation. Whereas ECWA is blessed with a wide range of preachers and teachers who are sound in the Word of God, there is also an urgent need to present the gospel in a way that would be appealing to many. The gospel itself is powerful and appealing, and so, its packaging must not be done in a manner that would compromise it or the integrity of the conveyor. The point here is that the gospel must be transmitted in ways that makes it attractive to its potential receivers. It is in this area that ECWA needs to engage in learning new skills.

ECWA can pick this challenge to learn new skills, especially in the area of effective appropriation of social media from the Pentecostals. I am sure the Pentecostals also have a lot to learn from ECWA as well. So, nothing is too much to sacrifice for the sake of the gospel of Christ. In their study of the relationship between Pentecostalism and the Nigerian Baptist Convention (NBC) Churches, Deji Aiyegbonyin and Emiola Nihinlola submit that 'No Nigerian church is an island unto herself. Baptist churches and Pentecostal churches are now positioned side by side in many parts of the country.'[25] And so the need to accommodate one another to the extent to which it is healthy for both sides is important. The opportunities in social media goes beyond platforms for preaching and teaching. It is now a major educational platform for learning, meetings, marketing, publicity, networking and many more. The mastery of these skills has contributed to the migration of our youth to these Pentecostal churches. The migration of young people to Pentecostal churches have been a major concern within the ECWA circles for a long time now. These studies have attracted a sizeable amount of research.

To my knowledge, some of the few published studies on this subject are those of John Omba Aina and Alao Joseph. Aina and Alao separately argue in their studies that the migration of youth from ECWA is caused by spiritual immaturity on the part of the youths, poor parenting, lack of sound biblical teaching, lack of understanding of the nature of youths, lack of welfare packages for the youth and lack of leadership opportunities and ambience – physical beauty of

---

[25] Deji Aiyegbonyin and Emiola Nihinlola, 'Pentecostalism and the Nigerian Baptist Convention Churches: The Way Forward' in *Ogbomosho Journal of Theology*, Vol. XIII (2) 2008, 224. (211-227)

other churches.[26] The factors are valid, but they are only few out of many other factors. New factors will emerge when empirical studies on the subject are conducted. Of all the factors mentioned by Aina, none points their possible attraction to the mastery of ICT and social media in other churches. Youths like to be affiliated to churches that have huge presence and visibility on social media.

But social media is not all that is important. Mature Christian youth are also attracted to sound biblical preaching and songs. This factor has also been responsible for the emigration of young people into ECWA. As a pastor of one of the local churches with the highest concentration of youths in ECWA, I have, on several occasions, witnessed the emigration of youth from Pentecostal churches into ECWA. That has been the case, in some instances, for young men marrying ladies from other church backgrounds or traditions. But in separate cases, I have seen individuals, couples and families of varied age groups, emigrate from other churches to ECWA. Oftentimes, the concern of leaders is on one side of the phenomenon – youth migration; more studies are needed to understand why young people from other denominations, especially Pentecostals, are emigrating to ECWA. The advice of Ayegboyin and Nihinola to NBC is equally appropriate for our reflection at this point. According to the duo, 'Since the Christian faith is living, it must grow; Baptist doctrine, as a living faith, must allow new reformations in line with contemporary spiritual yearnings and realities. While the NBC churches may endeavor to keep the Baptist identity and heritage, they should not be oblivious of the fact that the society in which Baptists live is not

---

[26] John Omba Aina, *How to Curb Youth Exodus from the Church* (Jos: Andex Press & Allied Services Limited, 2015), 24-32. See also Alao Oluwafemi Joseph, 'A Socio-Ethical Assessment of the Impact of Youth Migration on the Growth of Evangelical Church Winning All (ECWA), Lagos State' in *Net Journal of Social Sciences*, Vol. 5 (4) 2017, 68-77.

static.'[27] This truth applies not just to Baptists but also to ECWA. This must however be done under the guidance of the Word of God.

Going forward, the leadership of ECWA must be much more intentional and strategic in its approach to the appropriation of social media. Local churches at all levels should be made to appreciate the opportunities that lie in social media when used with discretion. Guided attention should be given to social media and the internet, generally on young and knowledge-based worshippers. This should have implications for the training of future leaders for the church. The theological education department in partnership with ECWA seminaries and Bible colleges should ensure that training in ICT and social media forms is a part of holistic theological education that speaks to its context.

Palliatives for the Less-fortunate Members

The weight of the financial stress caused by the coronavirus lockdown rests more on the less privileged in society. The coronavirus pandemic lockdown came with unquantifiable financial impacts on the nation, church and the common people. Poverty is a serious problem in Nigeria. Many Nigerians live on daily earnings that are less than $1 USD per day. One can only imagine the effects of the lockdown on the vulnerable. Members of ECWA were also affected. Federal and state governments, as well churches, organizations and well-to-do individuals in society stepped out to supply palliatives in the form of food items and token monies with the view of ameliorating the pain of the common people. Of course, there were challenges peculiar to our context regarding the faithful distribution of the materials to those who truly need them.

---

[27] Aiyegboyin and Nihinlola, 225.

Many Christian denominations were seen to be publicly involved in giving palliatives, not just to their members, but to the members of the public who may be in need of the same. ECWA was criticized for its low visibility in this regards to the distribution of palliatives at both the national and local levels. Many factors could be responsible for this. The trending practice of giving to the poor and blowing the trumpet on social media was against the teaching of the Bible (Matthew 6:1-2; 2:32-35). Being a Bible practicing denomination, this may be the reason why the performance of ECWA in supplying palliatives to the vulnerable was not as obvious at the national level as those of other churches. Besides, two additional factors could be responsible. How will a church survive giving palliatives to a population of over 10 million members? Given, the majority of these members may not need any. But those who could be in need would still have been significant.

What is the impact of this on the economy of the denomination? This was a demand that was heavy and unrealistic. For a denomination that depends largely on offerings and the generous giving of its members in order to operate, the ban on corporate worship that lasted for weeks (in Nigeria) made this distribution much more difficult. While responding to fake news insinuating that ECWA donated a huge sum of money to the government of Nigeria towards COVID-19, ECWA president, Rev. Stephen Panya Baba states:

> We hereby state that ECWA, as a church organisation, has many structures on ground... steering the ship of medical care, education, agriculture, broadcast industry and more. ECWA does not have any extra funds anywhere to donate to either federal or state governments. Should there have been funds, ECWA would rather strengthen the more these very useful

outfits of hers that were established in order to reach [the] most needy of the Nigerian populace . . . That is what ECWA leadership focuses on.

This leads us to ECWA's approach to the distribution of palliatives, which has to do with the administrative structure of the church.[28] ECWA utilizes the grassroots structural organization. The hierarchy of the church moves from the Local Church Board (LCB) level to the Local Church Council (LCC). The Local Church Council is headed by the Local Overseer (LO). The LCC is, in turn, responsible to the District Church Council (DCC). The DCC is under the leadership and supervision of an executive chairman and secretary. The DCC takes care of allocation of ministers to various churches. It is the highest authority in the district. Besides, the District Church Council is responsible to the General Church Council (GCC). The General Church Council is headed by the ECWA President.[29] ECWA operates a bottom-up administrative structure where power flows from the grassroots to the top. This is also how finances flow; twenty-five percent of the total income that comes to every local church (with few exceptions) goes up. Ten percent of the 25% is used for the operations and the management of the DCC office; while the remaining 15% goes to the headquarters. This structure allows for only local churches to care and minister to the needs of it vulnerable members. It is therefore the responsibilities of the LC (local church), LCC, DCC and GCC leaders to ensure that churches under their domains of leadership do not default in this assignment.

---

[28] Stephen Baba Panya, 'Updates on COVID-19 Pandemic by the ECWA President' in *ECWA eCommunicator:* https://www.ecwausa.com/2020/04/17/updates-on-covid-19-pandemic-by-the-ecwa-president-17-april-2020/ Posted on April 17, 2020, Accessed on April 28, 2020.

[29] E. A. Adeyemi, From Seven to Seven Thousand, 14-15.

The initiative of sending occasional letters of pastoral greetings to members by ECWA president during the lockdown is commendable. However, as good as this approach is, it appears weak and uncoordinated. In future, stringent monitoring strategies should be put in place by the GCC in order to ensure that vulnerable members of the church and of the society are cared for at all levels of the church, especially at the grassroots level. This has great implication for the future of the church. Members feel loved when cared for, especially in times of trouble. This is compatible with biblical teachings on love and with the evangelical position on holistic ministry of the church.

In this chapter, we have endeavoured to situate ECWA within it history and highlight its contributions to the sociopolitical development of Nigeria. We have also underscored areas where ECWA needs improvement in its response to the coronavirus lockdown, as well as offered insights for a better future.

CHAPTER NINE

IMPLICATIONS FOR THE CHURCH IN AFRICA

Our last three chapters have focused on ECWA, Nigeria. In those chapters, we briefly traced the history of ECWA and the essential elements of its corporate worship, as well as how it responded to the coronavirus lockdown. The coronavirus outbreak and the consequent lockdowns have so many implications for the global church. The concern of this final chapter is to highlight the lessons the wider church can glean from the responses of ECWA to the lockdown. Our focus here is on the church in Africa, especially the evangelical movement.

Implication for Evangelism and Technological Investment

The coronavirus pandemic has left the world in a permanently different shape. The changes are diverse and massive. It is no more business as usual. Fresh thinking, creative initiatives and novel approaches are now needed for the operation of most systems and organisations in the world. The words of Paul, *'The old has gone, the new is here!'* (2 Corinthians 5:17, NIV), are now not only true for the new life in Christ experience, but equally true for the operations of the post-coronavirus church. The church in Africa must now rethink its strategy for it to be able to fulfil its mission on earth within our new normal context. One of such turning points where the church must make decisive rethinking is in the area of evangelism. It was Henry Okullu who opined that, 'Christians must bring the gospel of light to the whole of humanity through evangelistic efforts. The church must attack lack of faith with faith and seek conversion to Jesus Christ, so that all men and women may come to accept him as Lord and Savior, both in their own personal lives and their corporate activities.'[1] How now shall the Church in Africa achieve this without investing in information communication technology (ICT)? The church needs to be intentional in this.

I laugh profusely whenever I recall an experience that I had some four years ago in relation to the relationship between the gospel and social media. Then, one of my church members approached me to counsel the leadership of a sister church in our city to stop the proceedings of their Sunday corporate worship services on Facebook.

---

[1] Henry Okullu, *Church and State in Nation Building and Human Development* (Nairobi: Uzima Press Limited, 1984), xvi.

According to him, the act was unconventional and demeaning to the gospel. He did not like the idea that a mainstream Evangelical church was toeing the path of the neo-Pentecostal-Charismatic denominations. Little did we know that that would be the order of the day for virtually all Christian denominations globally a few years later? The African church cannot close its eyes to the importance of ICT and media in our times. This is one of the takeaways of the lockdown. The virtual service served as an alternative channel for reaching and connecting with church members during the lockdown. It helped in reaching a wide range of audiences within a short period of time. This also helped in the spiritual pilgrimage of Christians, especially those at that time still struggling with being established in faith.

It is true that ICT and media have their own challenges. Firstly, it cannot, in some ways, replace corporate worship. The place of social interaction in corporate fellowship and worship of believers is irreplaceable. Secondly, it is capital intensive. The social and economic challenges, as well as infrastructural deficiency in Africa, makes the pursuit of the project daunting for most churches. This reality is not only so for the church as an entity but also for most members of the church as well. But is not it in the same continent that we have some denominations running universities, building some of the largest church auditoria in the world? So, this is not difficult for most churches in Africa where the leadership is intentional and determined.

Investment in ICT and media complement the effort of the church in evangelism, discipleship, and in information dissemination and management. Text messaging in indigenous or common languages may help in reaching disadvantaged demographics in a given context. This is particularly important for aged Christians and those living in rural contexts, since the majority of Africans now have access, at least, to mobile phones. The church could also lead in advocating for reduction of service charges on the general populace. The point here is that the role of ICT and media in complementing the efforts of the church in its evangelistic mandate cannot be not over-emphasised.

Implication for Ecumenism

Africans are renowned for their strong community ties and kinship networks. Despite the challenges posed by globalization over several years, the *Ubuntu* spirit of Africa has remained active and undefeated. The term *Ubuntu* originated from the Bantu people of Eastern and Southern African. It is a philosophy that has been variously used to express the united characteristic of the African people. The philosophy argues that there is 'a universal bond connecting all human beings, and that bond leads us to care for others and show humanity to all people.'[2] The spirit of *Ubuntu* promotes love, care and unity. It holds that no individual can succeed without the support of others – *'I am because you are.'* As such, the problem of one is the problem of all, and prosperity of one is the prosperity of all. This is supposed to be a commitment and a responsibility. It is, therefore, a *sin* to fail to offer help to a needy brother or sister when in position to do so.

Could this philosophy be the driving force behind pan-Africanism? Africa seemed to have been more united and achieved more politically and culturally through the efforts of pan-Africanists of the last century than what we have now. *Ubuntu* is a not a perfect philosophy. It has its own weaknesses and challenges. But it is a good portraiture of the biblical teachings on love, care, mercy and unity.

---

[2] John Jusu, eds. 'Ubuntu' in *Africa Study Bible* (Nairobi: Oasis International Limited, 2016), 1894.

Christians in the early church typified this for us. They viewed themselves as a family, bonded together by the love and course of Christ. Following this spirit, they shared everything they had in common (Acts 2:44–45; and 4:32–35). Without downplaying their individual peculiarities, they worshipped, ministered and confronted their challenges and shared in joys as one united community.

Regrettably, *Ubuntu* seems to have an insight only into the African culture and not into the church life of the African people. Taken, *Ubuntu* is only a philosophy. But what about the teaching of the Bible on Unity? The African church has never been more disintegrated than now. Of course, many factors are responsible for this. But chief among them is unhealthy denominationalism. This is one of the strongest enemies of the church in Africa. This challenge has weakened the very foundation of it, and it is not showing any sign of slowing down. We have denominational universities, hospitals, schools, banks, electricity companies and seminaries. Experience shows that there are denominational 'tongues' (glossolalia), sermons and *Bibles*. Even in the Evangelical movement, there are Christians who stereotype a whole denomination – viewing them all as unsaved. We have denominationalized virtually everything about Christian spirituality and practice, but the barrier is so thick. Most churches, left to themselves, do not want to have anything to do with others. This problem has fueled hatred and pride among denominations, as well as among their adherents. Denominationalism has scattered the collective resources of the African church and has weakened our capability to confront collective barriers. Sadly, this has reduced the potential of the church in ministering itself and has greatly reduced the impact of the Christian message in the public sphere.

However, the coronavirus lockdown brought a ray of hope to the church in Africa in relation to ecumenism. As it has been the case in her history, the leadership of ECWA mobilized its members to cooperate with directives given by the Christian association of Nigeria (CAN).[3] One such directive was when the leadership of CAN directed churches across the country to observe fasting and prayer from March 22–22, 2020 in order to contain the spread of the Coronavirus pandemic.[4] Being the largest and the most recognized Christian ecumenical body in Nigeria, its primary duties are that of representing the Christian body to the government and vice versa. Thus CAN plays an intermediary role between the church and the government. So, it is expected that CAN provides direction to the church on serious internal and public matters that might affect the collective wellbeing of the church.

As good as the mission of CAN appears, there are internal wrangles and denominational differences strong enough to challenge its health and mission, at times. Before the spate of COVID-19, we saw a harmonious relationship between CAN and ECWA.[5] This relationship was sustained even during the COVID-19 lockdown in Nigeria. This kind of relationship should not only be visible in times of crises. Whereas it is a daunting task to seek to make the church

---

[3] Stephen Baba Panya, 'Updates on COVID-19 Pandemic by the ECWA President' in *ECWA eCommunicator*. See also Peter Amine, 'COVID-19: ECWA Declares 3-Day Fasting and Prayer for God's Intervention' in *NNN*.

[4] 'Nigeria's Christian Association Declares National Prayers Over Coronavirus' in *Sahara Reporters*: http://saharareporters.com/2020/03/19/nigeria's-christian-association-declares-national-prayers-over-coronavirus/ Posted on March 19, 2020, Accessed on April 10, 2020.

[5] Stephen Baba Panya, 'Pray for the Persecuted Christians in Nigeria' in *ECWA eCommunicator*: https://www.ecwausa.com/2020/01/29/pray-for-persecuted-christians-in-nigeria/#menu-main-slide/ Posted on January 29, 2020, Accessed on April 10, 2020.

one in every sense and come together under a common framework, it is not impossible. In order to achieve this, emphasis should be placed on areas of commonalities, while areas of differences should be de-emphasised. This is not out of reach when there is mutual love, respect, understanding and tolerance. The challenges confronting the church in Africa are enormous and nuanced. Surmounting them will require collaborations, partnership, united initiatives and effort. Thanks to God for using the coronavirus lockdown to inject new hopes in us in this regard.

Implication for Prosperity Preaching

More often than not, when the issue of prosperity is mentioned, what comes to the mind of an average Nigerian, particularly Christians, is money or being materially rich. In other words, prosperity equates material wealth and financial capability. Is this surprising? I do not think so, especially because of the damage some preachers have done to the subject of prosperity. This line of thought is a product of the kind of teaching known technically as the prosperity gospel, where the proponents teach that health and material prosperity is a right of all believers in Jesus Christ. In other words, prosperity gospel teaches that all must be rich and that sin is the only factor that could prevent a Christian from being materially prosperous. Sadly, this misleading teaching has gained great popularity and wide acceptance by a major part of the church in Nigeria today. This teaching, rather than liberating the Church, is putting it in bondage and limiting the impact of the Christian message.

When listening to various sermons on the radio or television, and I reading in print media and on social media, I cannot help but think about how prosperity gospel has assumed a different dimension in Nigeria. Everywhere seems to have been permeated with the message of breakthrough and prosperity, which is undoubtedly promoting corruption. You hear, almost on a daily basis, of atrocities some people commit in the name of God while preaching their gospel of prosperity, and expectedly, the evils that men who have listened to the unbalanced sermons on prosperity perpetrate. As a matter of fact, it is no longer news that Nigeria is one of the most corrupt nations on today. The subject of corruption is the most talked about and strongest challenge facing the people and nation of Nigeria. Corruption is evident in virtually all the strata of Nigerian society.

Unfortunately, the church, which is the ground and pillar of truth –and should be the conscience of the society – has also been caught in the web of this deadly plague. The Christian fold is now divided on the definition of prosperity, as evidenced in the debate that broke out in Nigeria, following the news of the gift of a private jet given to Pastor Ayo Oritsejafor, a former president of the Christian Association of Nigeria (CAN), by members of his congregation on his birthday and 40th ordination anniversary.[6] The debate centered on the opulent lifestyles of some pastors within the Nigerian Pentecostal circles, as highlighted earlier in 2011 by *Forbes*, a popular American business and financial information magazine. The magazine published a list of some religious functionaries as the richest pastors in Nigeria. While some Nigerian social commentators see the acquisition of private jets and the display of opulence by some pastors, especially those belonging to the Pentecostal circles,

---

[6] Eghes Eyieyien, 'Of Nigerian Pastors and Private Jets,' *Vanguard Newspaper*: http://www.vanguardngr.com/2012/11/of-nigerian-pastors-and-private-jets/, Published on 23 November 2012, Accessed on Thursday 21 February, 2012.

as signs of divine prosperity, others see it as a dent on the image of the church.[7]

In any case, the proponents of the prosperity gospel, as being preached in Nigeria, promise their adherents almost anything and everything in the name of prosperity. They claim that Christ promised health and wealth by all means. Prosperity preachers argue that poverty in the lives of Christians can only be traced to sin, faithlessness and unbelief. Undoubtedly, poverty is one of the major crises confronting Nigeria today. While this is not a challenge peculiar to Nigeria and, indeed, Africa, the continent houses most of the poorest human beings on earth. Sadly, a recent study conducted by the Brookings Institution, a United States of American think tank, reveals that Nigeria is home to some of the poorest people on earth today. According to the report:

---

[7] MfonobongNsehe, 'The Five Richest Pastors in Nigeria,' *Forbes*: http://www.forbes.com/sites/mfonobongnsehe/2011/06/07/the-five-richest-pastors-in-nigeria/, Published: 6 June 2011, Accessed: 21 February, 2013. See also Phillip Eta, 'El-Rufai Mocks Pastor Oritsejafor on His New Private Jet,' *DailyPost Nigerian Online Newspaper*: http://dailypost.com.ng/2012/11/11/el-rufai-mocks-pastor-oritsejafor-new-private-jet/, Published: 11 November, 2012, Accessed: 22 February, 2013. See also Ogala Emmanuel, 'Obahiagbon joins Kuka, Bakare; blasts private jet owing pastors,' *Premius Times*: http://premiumtimesng.com/news/108522-obahiagbon-joins-kuka-bakare-blasts-private-jet-owning-pastors.html, Published on 25 November 2012, Accessed on 22 February, 2013. OseOyamendan, 'Our Jerry Curls Billonaire Pastors and Their Private Jets,' *Premium Times*: http://premiumtimesng.com/opinion/106709-our-jerry-curls-billionaire-pastors-and-their-private-jets-by-ose-oyamendan.html, Published: 12 November 2012, Accessed: 22 February, 2013; Uzor Maxim Uzoatu, 'Pastors of Private Jets and the Universal Church,' *Premium Times*: http://premiumtimesng.com/opinion/107979-pastors-of-private-jets-and-the-universal-church-by-uzor-maxim-uzoatu.html, Published: 21 November 2012, Accessed: 22 February, 2013. See Sunday Oguntola, 'Pastors with Private Jets: An Embarrassment,' *The Nation*: http://thenationonlineng.net/new/news/pastors-with-private-jets-an-embarrassment-bishop-kukah/, Published on 18 November, 2012, Accessed on February 22, 2013.

Nigeria, with the latest estimated population of 200 million, had overtaken India (1.32 billion population) as the poverty capital of the world. Specifically, it reported that with 87 million people already living below the poverty line, six new people fall into extreme poverty every minute.[8]

Because poverty has affected every aspect of Nigeria's national life, the church has had her share of the challenge, and since the Church cannot fold her arms in the face of this situation, she has looked for ways of responding to the unfortunate situation. One of the ways devised by some Church leaders to accomplish this goal, is by using the Word of God to give hope and encouragement to the people, and it was from there that the message of prosperity spread and increased. Prosperity preachers argue that the church should work hard to combat social, political and economic oppression in our society. The theology found its springboard on how Jesus Christ ministered to the poor and outcast in society.[9] While this is true, it is however unfortunate that, in the process of doing the above, many have misinterpreted and manipulated the Word of God to suit their purposes.

The *prosperity preachers* have also claimed that most people have refused to get their material prosperity and miracles because of faithlessness and unbelief. The fallout of these teachings is that they do not usually emphasize the supremacy of God on any issue as it relates to individuals and mankind as a whole. The very important issue of sin is not an important topic in the content of the prosperity

---

[8] 'Addressing Extreme Poverty in Nigeria' in *Vanguard:* https://www.vanguardngr.com/2018/09/addressing-extreme-poverty-in-nigeria/ Posted on 5th September, 2018, Cited on Thursday, 18th October, 2018.

[9] 'Prosperity Gospel' in Microsoft Encarta Premium Dictionary, 2009.

gospel theology. According to Samuel Abogunrin, 'the promises of material blessing by Yahweh were contingent on complete loyalty and obedience on the part of Israel. Unfortunately, today, the eager audience is fed with the great promises of God's abundant blessings, almost to the neglect of the conditions under which those blessings will flow.'[10] At this juncture, I'd like to say categorically and emphatically that God is not against the success of His people. But this should not be stressed above all other teachings of the Bible, which oftentimes serve as God's condition for prospering anyone.

The doctrine of prosperity is not only unrealistic but dangerous. It creates in Christians the extreme desire for wealth, whereas the emphasis of the Bible is on the dangers inherent with that kind of desire. Prosperity gospel, also, de-emphasises the doctrine of discipleship, which Jesus called for in every believer. The health and wealth gospel has to be reformatted and redefined. Its theological errors may have risen from a hermeneutical inadequacy, which takes the preachers interpret text out of context. The beginning of reformation, then, is attaining better theological training. Members should also be empowered to check the teaching of their leaders against the Word of God in order to hold on to that which is true.

The church in Africa has, apparently, become a toothless bulldog in the public sphere. This is because the church no longer enjoys the respect it used to have. Many church leaders are involved in the kind of fraudulent practices for which the majority of our political leaders are known. There is as much corruption in the church as there is outside it. However, sincere church leaders who remain the vanguards of the truth are like lone voices in the wilderness. The church is expected to respond to the problem of corruption and

---

[10] S. O. Abogunrin, *'Jesus Pronouncement on Wealth in the context of Prosperity gospel in Nigeria.'* Biblical Studies Series, Volume. 6, 2006. 241.

other myriads of social evils prominent in African society. And it is by doing this that the church can present the gospel of Jesus with the situation of the people in mind. However, these battles cannot be fought by a church that is, itself, corrupt, a church whose emphasis is on the *man of God* and material acquisitions, rather than Christ and living the life of Christ. Believers must emulate the humility and simplicity of Christ in all they do. The words of Evangelist Isaac Omolehin on a social media platform during the coronavirus lockdown in Nigeria is instructive for our reflection and conclusion of this subject:

> Build one mile church, no one goes there now for service. Build the largest church in the world, it is now empty. Buy [a] jet, fly nowhere now. We have been deceiving people for over 50 years. Prosperity, yes. But there is nowhere now to spend the money. The post-Coronavirus life in this world will not be the same anymore. Expect the same for the church...

This calls for a priority reset on the part of church leaders and those who continue to resist the Master and are sadly being swept away by the wind of this new normal. Prosperity gospel needs to incorporate the reality of Christian suffering into its theology. It also needs to respect the sovereignty of God over all human affairs. While it should continue to encourage Christians to seek divine intervention to their problems, it should avoid manipulating them by teaching that all forms of suffering come as a result of sin. What explanation can we give in the case of Job and other biblical characters that suffered a similar fate despite the outstanding testimonies given by the Word of God concerning them?

The Cross of Christ symbolises the suffering of Christ. It symbolises the sacrificial death that he suffered for the redemption of humankind. Discipleship in Jesus' view involves, not only self-denial and submission to the will of the Master, but also a call to endure inconveniences and discomfort as we partake of the redemptive suffering of Christ (Matthew 16:24; Luke 9:23). Partaking in his suffering does not come only in the form of persecution; the Christian may have to bear at times lack, sorrow and loss as part of his or her calling (Philippians 3:10; 2 Corinthians 1:5; 1 Peter 4:13). The coronavirus lockdown and the ban of public worship are a form of suffering that Christians are called to endure. Beyond the pain of the lockdown, there were several faithful Christians who tested positive to coronavirus around the world. While some were fortunate to come out of the woods, others had to pay the supreme price of death.

So, Christian suffering could manifest in diverse forms, part of which could come in forms of sickness and sometimes, death. Believers are expected to remain hopeful and faithful to Christ, even in the midst of life-threatening challenges (1 Thessalonians 4:13–14). God allows suffering in the lives of his children for so many reasons. One such reason, in the wisdom of James Montgomery Boice, is 'so that the world might know that our power is not from ourselves, but from God. The apostle Paul was repeatedly imprisoned, beaten, stoned, shipwrecked, starved, and threatened, but he never allowed these sufferings to reduce his love and commitment for Christ.'[11] Christians should always be able to say like Apostle Paul that: *'For to me, to live is Christ and to die is gain'* (Philippians 1:21, NIV). No one prays for suffering, but it does come. Suffering could even be self-inflicted. The Bible warns against self-inflicted suffering (1 Peter 4:15 and Galatians 6:7–9). But aside from

---

[11] James Montgomery Boice, *Come to the Waters: Daily Bible Devotions for Spiritual Refreshment* (Phillipsburg, New Jersey: P&R Publishing, 2017), April 30.

self-inflicted suffering, the Bible teaches that suffering could come in forms of persecution (1 Peter 4: 12–19; 2 Corinthians 11:16–33); divine discipline (Hebrew 12:5–11) and trials of faith. With the exception of the self-inflicted ones, all other forms of Christian suffering come mainly for the name of the Lord to be glorified (John 12: 1–3). Even self-inflicted suffering could culminate in giving glory to God. The outcome of the life of one of the criminals crucified alongside Jesus is a testimony to this possibility (Luke 23:39–43). Glorifying God at all times should be the primary goal of every Christian.

Implication for Holistic Discipleship

No subject should be more urgent for the church in Africa today than that of discipleship. Our daily realities confirm this need. The discipleship that I am proposing is not the common one that focuses on the laity and the clergy. Everyone irrespective of status in the church should be committed to the lifelong attachment to Christ. There should be strong teachings and emphasis on character formation and integrity. Integrity validates our message. Our actions demonstrate whether what we say is true or not. Because our message is Christ's message to the world, it is important that integrity and vitally are stressed. I am convinced that the gospel would have reached everyone in the world centuries ago if it were not for conflicting messages Christians have sent with actions that do not line up with the Word. We have all seen the Gospel message maligned because of the actions of someone who claimed to be a Christian. Many who have rejected the gospel do not actually have a problem with the Gospel but with the character of the individuals proclaiming it.[12] The words of Ted Haggard are succinct at this point: 'Faults in character will give the

---

[12] Haggard, *Your Primary Purpose*, 139.

devil a *place* in our lives that he will use to destroy our abilities to fulfill our primary purpose. It does not matter how spiritual we seem to other people. We would not fool the devil, and we cannot fool God. Remember: character counts!"[13]

Church leaders must live by example. Our lives are our credentials... and our influence on others depends most on who we are. Church leader should not just preach and teach their members on the necessity of godliness and a healthy relationship with God and fellow men, they must practicalize the same for others to see. Leaders are expected to be models and pacesetters, that is, they lead while others follow their example. Unfortunately, this is not always the case. It is a sad and disappointing phenomenon to see spiritual leaders whose lives are not worthy of emulation by their followers. Hence the need for holistic discipleship – involving both the laity and the clergy. The sudden shift in focus from the *God* of men or the people of God to the true owner of the church during the coronavirus lockdown should be a witness to our fragility. This calls for humility. It is high time we allowed the true owner of the church to occupy the center stage of his *property*. Our motives for ministry should not be different from that of John. '*He must become greater and greater, and I must become less and less*' (John 3:30, NLT). We have succeeded in idolizing ourselves when the reverse is the case. And not fame nor material prosperity, not power nor network, not even anointing nor *charisma* should take any one to that point. It can be dangerous.

Implication for Revival and Righteous-living

The world church urgently needs revival. But the need is even more urgent in Africa. Many factors are responsible for my submission.

---
[13] Ibid., 153.

Let me isolate a few. My first reason has to do with Africa being privileged to be one of the epicenters of the contemporary world of Christianity. God must have a reason for allowing this development to include Africa. I believe there is an expectation, both from God and the wider church, from the African church. Historian Andrew Walls appears to be prophetic when he declared: 'That Africa will bring gifts to the church is widely recognized, and many see those gifts as including a zeal for Christ, unembarrassed witness to him, energy and delight in worship, and fervency in prayer, all of which will bless the wider church but Africa must bring intellectual and theological leadership and authentic Christianity to the wider church too.'[14] Of all the three expectations of the global church on the African church, none, in my opinion is more urgent than authentic Christianity. While intellectual and theological leadership may be at par, authentic Christianity is at the foundation. This need concerns both the leaders of the church as well as their followers.

What are the implications of this shift for our theological and spiritual formation, for our church communities, for the marketplace and public spheres, for academia and for our witnesses to Christ, both locally and globally? Are believers and church leaders in Africa aware of this new dawn? Are church leaders prepared to participate in what God is doing in the world today? What are our roles and responsibilities as church leaders in Africa? How shall we achieve this in the midst of so many unbiblical practices going on in our environment? An illustration given to Richard Ramesh below explains the complexity better:

---

[14] Andrew F. Walls, World Christianity, 'Theological Education and Scholarship' in *Transformation: An International Journal of Holistic Mission Studies* in http://journals.sagepub.com/doi/full/10.1177/0265378811417514, Posted on September 12, 2011, Accessed on August 16, 2017.

> Economists working on a Christian version of "corporate social responsibility" are finding that drug addiction, prostitution, alcohol use and other crime is reduced in communities where churches are healthier. Church health impacts societal health. On the other hand, in 1994 Rwanda was the most "Christianized" country in Africa—some 90 percent of the people identified themselves as Christians. And yet, over a 100-day period, nearly 1 million people were killed in genocide there. It left the Hindu and Muslim worlds saying "if that is Christianity, we don't want anything to do with it." An unhealthy church—extremely superficial and easily turned from biblical Christianity—only reinforces the misperceptions non-believers have about Christianity. To have healthier churches we must have healthier pastors. To have healthier pastors, we connect, unite and strengthen trainers of pastors: the human core of pastoral effectiveness.[15]

The divinely orchestrated shift in the numeric heartlands of Christianity to the majority of the world calls for an urgent revival of righteous living on the parts of the church leaders and their followers. Revival does not just come. People must believe and pray for it. Part of the conditions for revival are humility, seeking the face of God in prayer and turning from wickedness (2 Chronicles 7:14). Sin affects our relationship with God. True repentance takes place when Christians humbly acknowledge their sins, forsake them and seek the face of God for forgiveness. One does not need a seer to

---

[15] Richard Ramesh, 'Global Proclamation Commission' in http://www.gprocommission.org/, Accessed on August 14, 2017.

see the reign of sin in African society. Sadly, many Christians have not lived above board in this regard. Many attend and are involved in church ministries, but the fruit of righteous living is not seen in them.

For now, COVID-19 remains a disease shrouded in mystery. Much would be known about it in the years ahead. But its lockdown has provided the opportunity for every Christian to retreat to Christ for the renewal of their commitments to righteous living. The effect of this could be seen in the outcome of our post-coronavirus living as individuals, the church and society. The light of our Christianity must shine beyond the confines of the church. Every strata of our *dark continent* must be lightened, seasoned and preserved by the impact of our *light* and *salt*. It is only the revival of righteous living that can make this possible. Only this transforms individual Christians and their communities. *Superficial Christianity* profits no one but Satan. It is our hope that the coronavirus lockdown serves the purpose for which God has allowed it in our lives, both as individuals and as a church.

BIBLIOGRAPHY

Abogunrin, S. O. 'Jesus Pronouncement on Wealth in the context of Prosperity gospel in Nigeria.' Biblical Studies Series, Volume. 6, 2006.

Adeboye, Albert Babajide. 'Effects of Industrial Revolution on Ecclesiastical Architecture in Nigeria: The Case of Faith Tabernacle at Ota' in *International Journal of Management, Information Technology and Engineering,* Vol. 3, Issue 2 (Feb., 2015), 28-34.

Adeleye, Femi. *Preacher of a Different Gospel.* Nairobi: HippoBooks, 2011.

Adeniyi, Olusegun. '"You are the Light of the World": The Church in the Public Eye.' The Third Vitality Lecture Delivered at the Centre for Biblical Christianity in Africa on Friday, June 7, 2019.

Adeyemi, E. A. *From Seven to Seven Thousand: The Story of the Birth and Growth of SIM/ECWA Church in Ilorin.*Ilorin: Okinbaloye Commercial Press, 1995.

Adeyemo, Tokunboh. 'Worship and Praise' in *Africa Bible Commentary,* Tokunboh Adeyemo, ed., Nairobi: WordAlive Publishers, 2006.

_____ . Tokunboh Adeyemo, 'Discipleship' *Africa Bible Commentary,* Tokunboh Adeyemo, ed., Nairobi: WordAlive Publishers, 2006.

Adogame, Afe. 'Online for God: Media Negotiation and African Religious Movements,' in *Who is Afraid of the Holy Ghost,* Afe Adogame, ed., (Trenton, NJ: Africa World Press, 2011), 223-235.

Aina, John Omba. *How to Curb Youth Exodus from the Church.* Jos: Andex Press & Allied Services Limited, 2015.

Aiyegboyin, Deji and Nihinlola, Emiola. 'Pentecostalism and the Nigerian Baptist Convention Churches: The Way Forward' in *Ogbomosho Journal of Theology,* Vol. XIII (2) 2008, 213-227.

Ajoku, Silent Aduche Frank. 'The Effects of Worship Practices in Pentecostal Church on Work Ethics in

Africa' in *Ogbomosho Journal of Theology,* Vol. XIII (2) 2008, 200-212.

Akinbami, Damilola. 'How Can Nigeria Withstand the Economic Impact of COVID-19?' In *Africa Business News,* April 12, 2020.

Alao, Oluwafemi Joseph. 'A Socio-Ethical Assessment of the Impact of Youth Migration on the Growth of Evangelical Church Winning All (ECWA), Lagos State' in *Net Journal of Social Sciences,* Vol. 5 (4) 2017, 68-77.

Anderson, Allan. *An Introduction to Pentecostalism.* Cambridge: Cambridge University Press, 2004.

Asamaoh-Gyadu, J. Kwabena. *'Born of Water and Spirit': Pentecostal/ Charismatic Christianity in Africa, Ogbu, U. Kalu,* ed., *in African Christianity: An African Story,* Series 5 Vol. 3 (Pretoria: Print Center, 2005), 387-409

_____ . 'Pentecostalism Media Images and Religious Globalization in Sub-Saharan Africa,' in *Belief in Media: Cultural Perspectives in Media and Christianity,* Peter Horsfield, Mary E. Hess, et. al., eds., (Hants, Ashgate, 2004), 65-67.

_____ . 'Mediating Spiritual Power: African Christianity, Transnationalism and the Media,' in *Religion Crossing Boundaries,* Afe Adogame and James V. Spickard, eds., (Boston: Brill, 2010), 87-103.

_____ . *Contemporary Pentecostal Christianity: Interpretations from an African Context.* Oxford: Regnum Books International, 2013.

Audi, Moses. 'Charismatic and Pentecostal Practices: An Introduction' in *Ogbomosho Journal of Theology,* Vol. XIII (2) 2008, Vi-Viii.

Bebbington, D.W. *Evangelicalism in Modern Britain: A History from the 1730s to the 1980s.* Oxfordshire: Routledge, 1989.

Bosch, David. *Transforming Mission: Paradigm Shifts in Theology of Mission.* Maryknoll, N.Y., Orbis Book, 1991.

Boice, James Montgomery. *Come to the Waters: Daily Bible Devotions for Spiritual Refreshment.* Phillipsburg, New Jersey: P&R Publishing, 2017.

Bounds, E.M. *Power Through Prayer.* Hobe Sound: Gospel Publishing Mission, 2000.

Brock, Naomi. 'Representations of Nigerian Women in Nollywood Films,' MA Thesis: Howard University, Washington (Dec., 2009).

Burgess, M. Stanley and Van Der Maas, M. Edwuard, eds. 'Charismatic Movement' In *The New International Dictionary of Pentecostal and Charismatic Movements.* Grand Rapids: Zondervan, 2003.

Burgess, Richard. 'Nigerian Pentecostal Theology in Global Perspective' *PentecoStudies,* Vol. 7, no.2, 2008, 29-63.

dela La Haye, Sophie. *Tread upon the Lion.* Ontario: Sudan Interior Mission, 1974.

Deng, Luka Biong. 'Social capital and civil war: The Dinka communities in Sudan's civil war,' *The Journal of the Royal African Society,* Volume 109, Number 435, April, 2010.

_____. 'Social Capital and Civil War: The Dinka Communities in Sudan's Civil War' *African Affairs: The Journal of the Royal African Society,* Volume 109, No. 435, April, 2009.

Douglas, J.D. and Cairns, E. Earle. "Charismata" In *The New International Dictionary of the Christian Church.* Grand Rapids: Zondervan Publishing House, 1978.

Douglas, Peterson Douglas, 'Latin *America Pentecostalism: Social Capital, Networks, and Politics*' (*PNEUMA: The Journal of the Society for Pentecostal Studies:* Volume 26, No 2, Fall 2004). 293-306.

Diara, C.D. Benjamin and Onah, G. Nkechinyere. 'The Phenomenal Growth of Pentecostalism in the Contemporary Nigerian Society: A Challenge to Mainline Churches' in *Mediterranean Journal of Social Sciences,* Vol. 5, No. 6 (April, 2014), 395-6.

Effa, F. Allan. 'Releasing the Trigger: The Nigerian Factor in Global Christianity' in *International Bulletin of Missionary Research,* Vol. 37, No. 4 (October 2013), 214-218.

Erickson, J. Millard J. Erickson, 'The Miraculous Gifts Today', In *Introduction Christian Doctrine.* Grand Rapids: Baker Academic, 2001.

Fakoya, Dayo. 'Gospel of Materialism-Nigerian Pentecostalism and Hypocrisy', *Tribune,* 28th August, 2008.

Falk, Peter. *The Growth of the Church in Africa.* Grand Rapids: Zondervan Publishing House, 1979.

Falola, Toyin, and Oyeniyi, Bukola Adeyemi. *Nigeria: Africa in Focus.* Santa Barbara: ABC-CLIO, 2015.

Fleck, Ian. *Bringing Christianity to Nigeria: The Origin and Work of Protestant Missions.* Bukuru: Africa Christian Textbooks, 2013.

Gifford, Paul. *Christianity, Development and Modernity in Africa.* London: Hurst & Company, 2015.

_____.*Christianity, Politics and Public Life in Kenya.* London: Hurst & Co., 2009.

_____. *Ghana's New Christianity. Pentecostalism in a Globalising African Economy.* London: Hurst & Company, 2004.

_____. *African Christianity: Its Public Role.* London: Hurst & Co., 1998

Grudem, Wayne. *Systematic Theology.* Nottingham: Inter-Varsity Press, 1994.

Haggard, Ted. *Your Primary Purpose: How to reach your Community and World for Christ.* Lake Mary: Florida, 2006.

Horby, A.S. "Worship" in Oxford Advanced Learner's Dictionary of Current English. Oxford: Oxford University Press, 2000.

Houston, M. James. "Spirituality" in *Evangelical Dictionary of Theology,* Walter A. Elwell, eds., Grand Rapids, Michigan: Baker Publishing Group, 2001.

Ihejirika, C. Walter. *From Catholicism to Pentecostalism: The Role Nigeria TelEvangelists in Religious Conversion* Port Harcourt: University of Port Harcourt Press, 2006.

_____. 'Research on Media, Religion and Culture in Africa: Current Trends and Dialogue,' *African Journal of Communication Research*, Vol. 2, No. 1 (2009), 1-60.

Isaac, John Paul. "Luke" in *Africa Bible Commentary*, Tokunboh Adeyemo, ed., Nairobi: WordAlive Publishers, 2006.

Isaacson, Alan. *Deeper Life: The Extraordinary Growth of the Deeper Life Bible Church*. London: Hodder and Stoughton, 1990.

Jatau, Audu Andrew and Kumnah, Banmang. 'Factors Associated with Internal Insecurity and the Impact on the Health of Families in Nigeria' *Nigerian Journal of Health Education*, Vol. 19 (1), 21-35.

Jenkins, Philip. *The Next Christendom: The Coming of Global Christianity*. Oxford: Oxford University Press, 2002.

Jusu John, eds. "Ubuntu" in *Africa Study Bible*. Nairobi: Oasis International Limited, 2016.

Kalu, U. Ogbu. *African Pentecostalism*. Oxford. Oxford University Press, 2008.

_____. 'Yabbing the Pentecostals: Paul Gifford's Image of Ghana's New Christianity,' African *Pentecostalism: Global Discourses, Migrations and Exchange and Connects*, Wilhelmina

J. Kalu, Nimi Wariboko, and Toyin Fabola, eds., Trenton, NJ: Africa World Press, Inc., 2010.

Kondracki, L. Nancy, et al., "Content Analysis: Review of Methods and Their Applications in Nutrition Education," *Journal of Nutrition Education and Behavior*, Vol. 34 (2002).

Kunhiyop, Waje Samuel. *African Christian Ethics*. Nairobi: World Alive Publishers, 2008.

Lumsdaine, H. David. 'Evangelical Christianity and Democratic Pluralism in Asia: An Introduction' in *Evangelical Christianity and Democracy in Asia*. David Halloran Lumsdaine, ed., Oxford: Oxford University Press, 2009, 3-42.

McDermott, R. Gerald. *God's Rivals: Insights from Biblical and Early Church*. Downer Groves: Inter-Varsity Press, 2007.

Marshall-Fratani, Ruth. 'Mediating the Global and the Local in Nigerian Pentecostalism,' *Journal of Religion in Africa*, Vol. 28, No. 3 (1998), 278-315.

Mwaura, Njeri Philomena. 'Gendered Appropriation of Mass Media in Kenyan Christianities: A Comparison of Two Women-Led African Instituted Churches in Kenya,' in *Interpreting Contemporary Christianity: Global Processes and Local Identities*, Ogbu U. Kalu, and Alaine Low, eds., Grand Rapids: William B. Eerdmans Publishing Company, 2008, 274-295.

Noll, A. Mark. *Between Faith and Criticism: Evangelical, Scholarship and the Bible in America*. San Francisco: Harper & Row, 1986.

Ogunyemi, Michael Olamide. *Problems and Challenges facing Higher Education Management in Nigeria: A Sociological and Philosophical Perspective.* Port Harcourt: Thaworld Global Resources Limited, 2003.

Okon, Godwin. 'Televangelism and Socio-Political Mobilization of Pentecostal in Port-Harcourt Metropolis: A KAP Survey,' in *Religion, Media and Politics in Africa,* No. 1 (Vol. V), 2011, 64-5.

Okullu, Henry. *Church and State in Nation Building and Human Development.* Nairobi: Uzima Press Limited, 1984.

Olatayo, D. I. *ECWA: The Root, Birth and Growth.* Ilorin: Ocare Publications Ocase Ltd. 1993.

Oladipo, Emmanuel. *Exemplary Christians in the Nigerian Public Square.* Ibadan: BLISS International Publishing, 2018.

Olowola, A. Cornelius. 'ECWA President's Address to the Participants of ECWA South-West Zonal Consultative Forum', at Ilorin, October 19, 2002.

Olufon, Wole. *Who is with you?* Lagos: Shalom Holdings and Ventures, 2002.

Oshatoba, S. A. 'Landmarks in the History of SIM/ECWA: An Analytical Approach,' Seminar Paper Presented at ECWA South-West First Zonal Convention at Ilorin, 19 October, 2002.

Otumala, Isaac. *Rudiments of Sociology.* Lagos: Sunkorin Enterprises, 2013.

Parker, David. 'Evangelical Spirituality Reviewed,' *Evangelical Quarterly* 63:2 (1991), 129-31.

Pinnock, H. Clark. "What Is Biblical Inerrancy?" in *Proceedings of the Conference on Biblical Inerrancy 1987.* Nashville: Broadman, 1987.

Putnam, D. Robert and Goss A. Kristin. "Introduction" in *Democracies in a Flux: The Evolution of Social Capital in Contemporary Society,* ed. Robert D. Putnam. Oxford: Oxford Press, 2002.

Rigobert, Kamate. 'Pentecostalism in Kinshasa: Maintaining Multiple Church Membership, Tanzania,' in *African Communication Research,* Vol. 2, No. 1, 2009.

Shaw, Mark *Global Awakening: How 21st Century Revivals Triggered a Christian Revolution.* Downers Grove: IVP Academic, 2010.

Stanley, Brian. *The Global Diffusion of Evangelicalism.* Nottingham: Inter-Varsity Press, 2013.

Stark, Rodney. *The Rise of Christianity: a Sociologist Reconsiders History.* New Jersey: Princeton University Press, 1996.

Stott, John. *The Contemporary Christian.* Leicester, UK: 2004.

Stott, R.W. John. *The Message of Acts.* Leicester: Intervarsity Press, 1990.

Tozer, A.W. 'The First Obligation of the Church,' *Herald of His Coming,* (January 2002).

Ukah, Asonzeh. *A New Paradigm of Pentecostal Power: A Study of the Redeemed Christian Church of God in Nigeria.* Trenton, NJ: Africa World Press, Inc., 2008.

_____. 'Advertising God: Nigerian Christian Video-Films and the Power of Consumer Culture,' *Journal of Religion in Africa*, Vol. 33, No. 2, Religion and the Media (May. 2003), 203-231.

_____. 'Banishing Miracles: Politics and Policies of Religious Broadcasting in Nigeria,' *Journal of Politics and Religion in Africa*, Vol. 1, No. 5, Religion, Media and Politics in Africa (2011), 39-59.

Varin, Caroline. *Haram and the War on Terror.* Santa Barbara: ABC-CLIO, 2016.

Wagner, Peter and Thompson, Joseph. *Out of Africa: How the Spiritual Explosion among Nigerians Is Impacting the World.* Ventura: Regal Books, 2004.

Walls, Andrew. *The Missionary Movement in Christian History: Studies in the Transmission of Faith.* Maryknoll, New York: Orbis Books, 1996.

_____. *The Cross-Cultural Process in Christian History.* Maryknoll, New York: Orbis Books, 2002.

Waribiko, Nimi. *Nigerian Pentecostalism.* Rochester, NY: University of Rochester Press, 2014.

Webster, N. "Indigenous" in *The New Webster's Dictionary of the English Language* ed. by Lawrence T. Lorimer et al., New York: Lexicon Publication, Inc., 1995.

Whitney, S. Donald. *Spiritual Discipline for Christians*. Colorado Springs: NavPress, 1997.

ECWA Books

ECWA Minister's Handbook, Jos: Challenge Press, 2002.

Bye-Laws of the Evangelical Church Winning All (As Amended 2019), Jos: ECWA Headquarters, 2019.

Constitution of the Evangelical Church Winning All (As Amended 2019), Jos: ECWA Headquarters, 2019.

Websites

'Addressing Extreme Poverty in Nigeria' in *Vanguard:* https://www.vanguardngr.com/2018/09/addressing-extreme-poverty-in-nigeria/ Posted on 5th September, 2018, Cited on Thursday, 18th October, 2018.

Akanni, Lateef Olawale and Gabriel Samuel Chukwudi. 'Of COVID-19 Pandemic on the Nigerian Economy' in *Centre for the Study of the Economies of Africa (CSEA)*: http://cseaafrica.org/the-implication-of-covid19-on-the-nigerian-economy/ Accessed on April 29, 2020.

American Addiction Resource Centers (2020) 'Drinking Alcohol While Working from Home' in *Alcohol.org: An American Centers Resources Alcohol Consumption:* https://www.alcohol.org/guides/work-from-home-drinking/ 2020, Accessed on April 29, 2020.

Amine, Peter. 'COVID-19: ECWA Declares 3-Day Fasting and Prayer for God's Intervention' in *NNN*: https://nnn.com.ng/covid-19-ecwa-decalares-3-day-fasting-prayers-for-gods-intervention/ Posted on March 31, 2020, Accessed on April 10, 2020.

Asunloye, Ademola.'Spotlight on Nigeria's Telecommunications Sector' in *Business Day*: https://businessday.ng/business-economy/article/spotlight-on-nigerias-telecommunications-sector/Posted on October 24, 2019, Accessed on April 16, 2020.

Ayeni, Tofe. 'Coronavirus: Nigeria's Varied Responses to Controlling COVID-19' in *theafricareport*: https://www.theafricareport.com/27773/coronaviru-nigerias-varied-responses-to-controlling-covid-19/ Posted May 13, 2020, Accessed on June 2, 2020.

Baba, Panya Stephen. 'ECWA President's Easter 2020 Speech' in https://youtu.be/DGtHY4nqBnw/ Accessed on April 18, 2020.

'Current Health Expenditure per Capita (Current US$) | Data.' Word Health Organisation Global Health Expenditure Database in *The World Bank:* 2015. https://data.worldbank.org/indicator/SH.XPD.CHEX.PC.CD/ Accessed April 25, 2020.

'ECWA President's Easter 2020 Speech' in *Truth and Honour* https://ama924.wordpress.com/2020/04/06/ecwa-presidents-easter-2020-speech/?fbclid=IwAR2EiComCAoArz0uBFYoc9Qok_5iq0RN7dM3Sv2yjrtqnsaAN6-xRFg0wcY/ Posted on April 6, 2020 by Amah-Kabong.

Balcomb, A.O. 'Evangelicalism in Africa: What it is and What it Does' in *Southern African Journal of Missiology: Missionalia* (Online),

Vol. 44, No 2, (Pretoria 2016)inhttp://www.scielo.org.za/scielo.php?script=sci_arttext&pid=S0256-95072016000200002, Cited on Tuesday 18 June, 2019.

Brown, Angie. 'Edinburgh Church Congregation Grows under Lockdown' in BBC News: https://www.bbc.com/news/uk-scotland-edinburgh-east-fife-52262025/ Posted April 12, 2020, Accessed on April 16, 2020.

'Christian Movements and Denominations' in *Pew Research Center Religion and Public Life*:http://www.pewforum.org/2011/12/19/global-christianity-movements-and-denominations/ Posted on 19th December, 2011; Accessed on 28th September, 2016.

'Coronavirus: Why Some Nigerians are Gloating About COVID-19' in *BBC*: https://www.bbc.com/news/world-africa-52372737/ Posted on April 23, 2020, Accessed on June 1, 2020.

'ECWA Church Lunches TV Station' in *The Nation*: https://thenationonlineng.net/ecwa-church-lunches-tv-station/ Posted on June 3, 2018, Accessed April 13, 2020.

'ECWA TV Africa: Our Core Values and Beliefs' in *ECWA TV*: http://ecwatv.org/about-us/ Accessed on April 16, 2020.

Emmannuel, Ogala. "Obahiagbon joins Kuka, Bakare; blasts private jet owing pastors," *Premius Times*: http://premiumtimesng.com/news/108522-obahiagbon-joins-kuka-bakare-blasts-private-jet-owning-pastors.html, Published on 25 November 2012, Accessed on 22 February, 2013.

Eta, Phillip. 'El-Rufai Mocks Pastor Oritsejafor on His New Private Jet,' *DailyPost Nigerian Online Newspaper*: http://dailypost.com. ng/2012/11/11/el-rufai-mocks-pastor-oritsejafor-new-private-jet/, Published: 11 November, 2012, Accessed: 22 February, 2013.

Eyieyien, Eghes. 'Of Nigerian Pastors and Private Jets,' *Vanguard Newspaper*: http://www.vanguardngr.com/2012/11/of-nigerian-pastors-and-private-jets/, Published on 23 November 2012, Accessed on Thursday 21 February, 2012.

Fakoya, Olusegun. 'The Gospel of Materialism – Nigerian Pentecostalism and Hypocrisy,' in *NVS*, in http://www.nigeriavillagesquare.com/article/dr-olusegun-fakoya/the-gospel-of-materialism-nigerian-pentecostalism-and-hypocrisy.html, posted on August 26, 2008, Accessed on July 9, 2015.

Finn, Nathan. 'On Evangelical Spirituality' in http://www.nathanfinn.com/2013/03/28/on-evangelical- spirituality/ Posted on March 28, 2013.

_____. 'Is there a Difference between Religion and Spirituality' in *Compelling Truth*: https://www.compellingtruth.org/difference-religion-spirituality.html/ Accessed on April 11, 2020.

Gachuki, Daniel. '3 Reasons Not to Support Conspiracy Theories' in *The Gospel Coalition Africa*: https://africa.thegospelcoalition.org/article/why-you-shouldnt-support-conspiracy-theories/ Posted on May 12, 2020, Accessed on June 1, 2020.

George, Taiwo. 'Only 37 Million Households in Nigeria have access to Television' in *TheCable*: https://www.thecable.

ng/37-million-households-nigeria-access-television/ Posted on September 16, 2020, Accessed on April 30, 2020.

Horgan, John Horgan. 'Antonine Plague' in *Ancient History Encyclopedia*: https://www.ancient.eu/Antonine_Plague/ Published on May 2, 2019.

_____. 'The Plague of Cyprian, 250-270 C'" in https://www.ancient.eu/article/992/plague-of-cyprian-250-270-ce/ Published December 13, 2016; Accessed on May 5, 2020.

Ifijeh, Martins. 'Nigeria Has Only 42,000 Doctors to 200 Million People, NMA President Cries Out' in *AllAfrica*: https://allafrica.com/stories/201912190053.html/ Posted on December 19, 2020; Accessed on May 2, 2020.

Igomu, Tessy. 'I didn't Know Nigeria's Health Sector was this Bad' in *Punch HealthWise*: https://healthwise.punch.com/i-did-know-nigerias-health-sector-was-this-bad-boss-mustapha/ Posted on April 10, 2020, Accessed on June 1, 2020.

Jegede, Olugemiro. 'COVID-19: ODeL Will Change World's Landscape of Teaching, Learning' in *Thisday*: https://www.thisdaylive.com/index.php/2020/04/08/covid-19-odel-will-change-worlds-landscape-of-teaching-learning/ Posted on April 8, 2020, Accessed on April 9, 2020.

Jewell, Tim. 'Everything you should know about the 2019 Coronavirus and COVID-19' in *Healthline*: https://www.healthline.com/health/coronavirus-covid-19/ Posted on April 23, 2020; Accessed on April 25, 2020.

Kripphl, Christian. 'Nigerian Religious Leaders Demand Lifting of COVID-19 Lockdown' in *DW*: https://m.dw.com/en/nigerian-religious-leaders-demand-lifting-of-covid-19-lockdown/a-53499533/ Posted on May 5, 2020, Accessed on June 2, 2020.

Kwushue, Mayowa. 'Coronavirus: Pastor Chris Makes Fearful Revelations about the COVID-19, New Vaccine, and AntiChrist' in *Nigeria News World*: https://nigerianewsworld.com/news/coronavirus-pastor-chris-makes-fearful-revelations-about-covid-19-new-vaccine-5g-antichrist-video/ Posted on April 5, 2020, Accessed on June 1, 2020.

Liverpool, Layal. 'Coronavirus: What is social distancing and do you do it?' in *NewScientist*: https://www.newscientist.com/article/2237664-coronavirus-what-is-social-distancing-and-how-do-you-do-it/ Posted on March 17, 2020, Accessed on April 12, 2020.

"Lockdown" in https://www.merriam-webster.com/dictionary/lockdown, Accessed on April 12, 2020.

Mathis, David. 'Five Benefits of Corporate Worship' in *DesiringGod*: https://www.desiringgod.org/articles/five-benefits-of-corporate-worship/ Posted May 25, 2014, Accessed on April 12, 2020.

Mbewe, Conrad. 'Why There is no such Thing as African Christianity' in https://www.9marks.org/article/why-theres-no-such-thing-as-african-christianity/ Accessed on June 24, 2019.

NOI-Polls 'COVID-19 Poll Result Release' in https://noi-polls.com/covid-19-poll-result-release/ Posted on March 18, 2020 and Accessed on April 29, 2020.

'Nigeria's Christian Association Declares National Prayers Over Coronavirus' in *Sahara Reporters*: http://saharareporters.com/2020/03/19/nigeria's-christian-association-declares-national-prayers-over-coronavirus/ Posted on March 19, 2020, Accessed on April 10, 2020.

Nsehe, Mfonobong. 'The Five Richest Pastors in Nigeria,' *Forbes*: http://www.forbes.com/sites/mfonobongnsehe/2011/06/07/the-five-richest-pastors-in-nigeria/, Published: 6 June 2011, Accessed: 21 February, 2013.

'Number of Evangelicals worldwide' in *Lausanne Movement* on https://www.lausanne.org/lgc-transfer/number-of-evangelicals-worldwide, Accessed on June 22, 2019.

Nwokoji, Chima. 'IMF Projects Negative GDP Growth for Nigeria in 2020' in *Nigerian Tribune Newspaper*: https://tribuneonlineng.com/imf-projects-negative-gdp-growth-for-nigeria-in-2020/ Posted on April 14, 2020, Accessed on April 29, 2020.

Oguntola, Sunday. 'Pastors with Private Jets: An Embarrassment,' *The Nation*: http://thenationonlineng.net/new/news/pastors-with-private-jets-an-embarrassment-bishop-kukah/ Posted on 18 November, 2012, Accessed on February 22, 2013.

Osuagwu, Prince. 'Nigeria: COVID-19, 5G Mix-Up – Why Nigerians are Worried' in *allAfrica*: https://allafrica.com/

stories/202004080125.html/ Posted on April 8, 2020, Accessed on June 1, 2020.

Owojaiye, Moses. The Problem of False Prophets in Africa in *Lausanne Global Analysis,* Volume 8, Issue 6 (November 2019): https://www.lausanne.org/content/lga/2019-11/problem-false-prophets-africa/ Accessed April 10, 2020.

Oyamendan, Ose. 'Our Jerry Curls Billonaire Pastors and Their Private Jets,' *Premium Times*: http://premiumtimesng.com/opinion/106709-our-jerry-curls-billionaire-pastors-and-their-private-jets-by-ose-oyamendan.html, Published: 12 November 2012, Accessed: 22 February, 2013;

Pastor Chris, '5G is Lovely But' in https://youtu.be/lXnLwtAS6Fk/ Posted on April 8, 2020.

"Plague" in *World Health Organization*: https://www.who.int/news-room/fact-sheets/detail/plague/

Posted on October 31, 2017, Accessed on May 5, 2020.

"Prayer with us" in https://www.sim.org/pray-with-us/ Accessed on April 13, 2020.

'Procedure for Obtaining License' in *National Broadcasting Commission:* https://www.nbc.gov.ng/pages/licensing/ Accessed on April 16, 2020.

"Prosperity Gospel" in Microsoft Encarta Premium Dictionary, 2009.

Ramesh, Richard. 'Global Proclamation Commission' in http://www.gprocommission.org/, Accessed on August 14, 2017.

Robertson, David. 'What is the Impact of Churches Closing Because of Coronavirus?' in *Christianity Today:* https://www.christianitytoday.com/article/what-is-the-impact-of-churches-closing-because-of-coronavirus/134477.htm/ Posted on March 18, 2020, Accessed on April 16, 2020.

Schumacher Traci. '5 Beliefs that Sets Evangelical Apart from other Christians' in https://www.newsmax.com/fastfeatures/evangelical-christians-beliefs/2015/04/02/id/636050/ Posted April 2, 2015.

Soyombo, Fasayo. 'The Grand Coronavirus Cover-Up in Kwara' in https://www.thecable.ng/the-grand-coronavirus-cover-up-in-kwara, Posted on April 6, 2020, Accessed on April 8, 2020

Stone, Lyman. 'Christianity Has Been Handling Epidemics for 2000 Years' in *Foreign Policy*: https://foreignpolicy.com/2020/03/13/christianity-epidemics-2000-years-should-i-still-go-to-church-coronavirus/ Posted on March 13, 2020, Accessed on May 5, 2020.

Sunquist, W. Scott. 'Attentiveness: Pandemic': *Gordon Conwell Theological Seminary*: https://www.gordonconwell.edu/blog/pandemic/ Posted on March 12, 2020; Accessed on May 5, 2020.

Ukah, Asonzeh. 'Building God's City: The Political Economy of Prayer Camps in Nigeria' in *International Journal of Urban and Regional Research* (Sept., 2016), Access on www.wiley.com/doi/10.1111/1468-2427/full.

Uzoatu, Maxim Uzor. 'Pastors of Private Jets and the Universal Church,' *Premium Times*: http://premiumtimesng.com/opinion/107979-pastors-of-private-jets-and-the-universal-church-by-uzor-maxim-uzoatu.html, Published: 21 November 2012, Accessed: 22 February, 2013.

Viner, M. Russell, Russell J. Simon, Croker, Helen. 'School Closure and Management Practices during Coronavirus Outbreaks including COVID-19: A Rapid Systematic Review' in *The Lancet Child and Adolescent Health Journal*, Vol.4, Issue 5 (May 01, 2020), published on April 6, 2020: https://www.thelancet.com/journals/lanchi/article/PIIS2352-4642(20)30095-X/fulltext/ 397-404, Accessed on April 29, 2020.

Walls, F. Andrew. World Christianity, 'Theological Education and Scholarship' in *Transformation: An International Journal of Holistic Mission Studies* in http://journals.sagepub.com/doi/full/10.1177/0265378811417514, Posted on September 12, 2011, Accessed on August 16, 2017.

Watts, Edwards. 'What Rome Learned from the Deadly Antonine Plague of 165 A.D' in *Smithsonian Magazine*: https://www.smithsonianmag.com/history/what-rome-learned-deadly-antonine-plague-165-d-180974758/ Published on April 28, 2020, Accessed on May 5, 2020.

Weigel, George. 'World Christianity by the Numbers' in *First Thing*:https://www.firstthings.com/web-exclusives/2015/02/world-christianity-by-the-numbers, Posted 25th February, 2015, Accessed on 28th September, 2016.

'What is social capital?' in http://www.wisegeek.com/what-is-social-capital.htm/ Accessed on December 1, 2010.

'What is social capital?' in Organization for Economic Co-operation and Development (OECD) Insight: http://www.oecd.org/dataoecd/36/6/37966934.pdf/ Accessed on December 1, 2010.

Yong, Amos. 'Evangelical, Pentecostals and Charismatics: A Difficult Relationship or Promising Convergence?' in *Fuller Studio: https://fullerstudio.fuller.edu/evangelicals-pentecostals-and-charismatics/* Accessed on April 9, 2020.

SCRIPTURE REFERENCE

Genesis
3
18:19

Exodus
23:1
35:21, 26, 29; 36

Joshua
Joshua 24:15

1 Kings
17:7-16

1 Chronicles
12:32

19:14
29:14

2 Chronicles
7:14

Job
1:5

Psalm
112:9

Proverbs
21:31
22:9
31:29

Jeremiah
29:7

Matthew
2:11
2:32-35
5:16
5:43-47
6:1-2
6:1-4
11:28-30
14:17
14:23
16:24
22:21

22:37-39
26: 36, 39, 42, 44
28:18-20

Mark
1:35
6:46
14:3-19
14:32, 35

Luke
5:16
6:12
6:46
9:18
9:23
13:32
21:1-4
23:39-43

John
3:16
3:30
4:24
8:31-36
12: 1-3
13:34-35

Acts
2:44-45
2:46

4: 1-47
4:32-35
4:34-35
5:1-11
5:42
5:29
7:54-60
8:1
8:3
10:22
16:32, 40
20:1-3
20:20
28:16, 30

Romans
8: 31-32
8:35-39
12:1-2
13:1-17
16:5

1 Corinthians
15:31
16:19

2 Corinthians
1:5
5:10
8:5
8:7

8:11
9:7
9:8
11:16-33

Galatians
6:7-8
6:7-9

Ephesians
5:23, 25-33
6:4

Philippians
1:21
2:3-11
4:22
3:10

Colossians
4:15

1 Thessalonians
4:13-14
5:21

1 Timothy
1:6
2:1-2
3:4-5

2 Timothy	James	2 Peter
3:5	1:27	2:13-17

Philemon	1 Peter	Revelation
1-25	2:13-17	1:8
	4:2	1:9
Hebrews	4:13	13
10:25	4:15	
13:8	4: 12-19	
12:5-11		

GENERAL INDEX

A

academic 3, 6, 32
activistic 54, 97, 99
African Christianity 37, 65, 68, 133
Airport 5
Aladura 17
Alexikakos 13
alien 28, 48
Anglican 36, 64
annals 89
Antonine 12, 13, 14, 15, 180, 185
apolitical 69, 132
auditorium 66
avaricious 89
Azusa Street 16, 55, 56

B

banditry 27, 52, 115
Baptist x, 36, 77, 128, 141, 142, 166
Bida 130
Boko-haram 27
Boko Haram 63, 91, 115
bona fide 95
Bonds 135
born-again 2, 42, 46, 54, 94, 99
Bridges 135
briefing 4, 5
Bulletins 78

C

CAN ix, 152, 154
capricious 14

cardinal 42, 44, 57
Catholic 36, 53, 61, 70
Catholicism 47, 70, 71, 171
cattle rustling 115
central 1, 42, 44, 46, 49, 53, 54, 57, 63, 71, 72, 77, 81, 88
century 7, 35, 53, 55, 60, 61, 124, 128, 150
challenge 27, 31, 54, 61, 98, 108, 109, 121, 140, 141, 151, 152, 154, 155, 156
charisma 55, 58, 77, 161
Charismatic 36, 53, 54, 57, 58, 59, 61, 62, 65, 70, 72, 80, 96, 140, 149, 167, 168
Christianity ix, xii, 3, 13, 14, 16, 17, 35, 37, 38, 39, 40, 41, 42, 43, 50, 51, 53, 54, 56, 57, 58, 59, 60, 61, 62, 64, 65, 67, 68, 69, 70, 71, 72, 73, 74, 76, 80, 82, 86, 89, 99, 103, 109, 113, 114, 116, 119, 120, 123, 124, 126, 132, 133, 162, 163, 164, 165, 167, 169, 170, 171, 172, 174, 181, 184, 185
Christlike 46
commercialization 52, 69, 70
commonwealth 98
Congregational Prayer 78
conjunctival 15
conspiracy 5
consumers 69

contemporary 7, 16, 40, 53, 66, 78, 79, 80, 86, 92, 98, 111, 131, 142, 162
continents 64
contraceptive 27
Convergence Theory 70
conversion 3, 42, 43, 46, 59, 148
convert 14, 72
Coronavirus 3, 4, 5, 6, 7, 8, 9, 10, 12, 31, 32, 33, 35, 76, 101, 102, 103, 107, 110, 111, 112, 113, 114, 115, 119, 120, 122, 125, 127, 140, 143, 146, 147, 148, 152, 153, 158, 159, 161, 164, 180, 181, 184, 185
corporate 3, 9, 74, 76, 77, 78, 79, 80, 81, 82, 102, 103, 104, 109, 110, 113, 116, 120, 127, 139, 144, 147, 148, 149, 163, 181
corruption 30, 52, 89, 115, 119, 154, 157
COVID-19 3, 4, 5, 6, 7, 8, 9, 10, 11, 12, 17, 18, 23, 24, 25, 26, 27, 29, 30, 31, 68, 75, 76, 100, 102, 103, 109, 110, 115, 116, 121, 126, 127, 134, 166, 176, 180, 182, 185
credibility 17, 52
crises 7, 12, 17, 32, 152, 155
Cyprian 14, 15, 180

D

deliverance 72, 125

demography 86, 105
denomination 9, 76, 77, 81, 83, 85, 88, 90, 91, 92, 95, 107, 109, 128, 131, 132, 138, 139, 140, 144, 149, 151
denominationalism 151
destructive 76
devastating 12, 26, 30, 111, 129
dichotomy 50, 134
discipleship 47, 52, 85, 93, 97, 117, 119, 132, 149, 157, 160, 161
Discipleship 85, 118, 119, 159, 160, 166
discouragements 130
discourse 7, 37, 70
Disease x, 3, 10
disintegrated 151
disruptive 76
doctrinal 36, 54, 55, 57, 61, 94, 95, 104
dramatized 3

E

Early Church 61, 98, 114, 120, 151, 172
ecclesia 37, 44
ecstatism 79
ecumenical 128, 133, 152
ecumenism 110, 152
Ecumenism 150
ECWA ix, x, xii, 3, 9, 36, 76, 77, 78, 79, 80, 81, 83, 84, 85, 86, 87, 88, 89, 90, 91, 92, 93, 94, 95, 97, 98, 99, 100, 102, 103, 104, 107, 108, 110, 111, 112, 113, 115, 116, 119, 121, 122, 124, 125, 126, 127, 128, 129, 130, 131, 132, 134, 138, 139, 140, 141, 142, 143, 144, 145, 146, 147, 152, 166, 167, 173, 176, 177, 178
ECWA TV 87, 103, 104, 107, 122, 132, 139, 178
emerging 14, 40, 70
Emotionalism 79
Emperor 12
empirical 72, 74, 142
environment xii, 2, 138
Ephesian 40
epicenter 10, 40, 63, 66
epidemic 11
epistemologies 133
ethos 36, 45, 48, 49, 51, 54, 57, 82
Europe 15
evangelical 3, 8, 36, 41, 42, 43, 44, 45, 47, 48, 49, 55, 76, 82, 83, 86, 90, 131, 132, 146, 147, 179, 184
Evangelical ix, x, 2, 3, 9, 35, 36, 41, 43, 44, 45, 46, 47, 48, 49, 51, 52, 54, 55, 56, 57, 82, 83, 85, 86, 87, 88, 97, 99, 102, 114, 116, 123, 124, 126, 128, 131, 142, 149, 151, 167, 170, 172, 174, 176, 179, 184, 186
Evangelical Christianity 3, 9, 41, 57

evangelicalism 36, 41, 45, 48, 55
Evangelicalism 16, 35, 41, 42, 53, 54, 55, 57, 63, 168, 174, 177
evangelism 14, 17, 42, 48, 79, 86, 88, 92, 93, 122, 132, 148, 149
evangelization 43, 85
evil 72, 87, 114
examination 1, 52, 95
exanthema 13
Executive 3, 95
exorcism 17, 58
explosion 53, 65, 66
extra-judicial killings 115
extremists 115

F

fatalism 115
Federal x, 4, 24, 25, 32, 103, 112, 143
film 2, 68, 69, 73, 74
flamboyance 73
Forbes 154, 155, 182
foreseen 111
frail 8

G

Garku 130
gastrointestinal 13
gathering 4, 8, 11, 101, 103, 112, 113
genealogy 55

global 3, 7, 9, 10, 12, 16, 17, 26, 28, 31, 32, 35, 39, 40, 56, 61, 67, 86, 91, 112, 125, 147, 162, 178
glossolalia 54, 58, 59, 151
Governor 3, 5
Greek 13, 48, 58, 82

H

healing 17, 58, 125
heartlands 39, 40, 163
heretical 88, 89
hermeneutical 55, 133, 157
Hierapolis 13
Historians 12, 13
HIV/AIDS 6, 133
holiness 46, 47, 51, 56
holistic 50, 134, 143, 146, 161
Hospital x, 4
humankind 45, 97, 159
Hymn Singing 78

I

ICT x, 74, 105, 139, 142, 143, 148, 149
idolize 45
Ilorin x, xii, 3, 4, 5, 86, 108, 129, 166, 173
immobility 24
Implication 139, 148, 150, 153, 160, 161
indelible 8
index 3, 4, 76, 180
indigenous 40, 63, 70, 93, 131, 149

infectious 6
inflation 24, 32
ingenuity 8
innovative 134
instructive 29, 51, 89, 101, 158
intermediary 152
International x, xii, 5, 26, 59, 64, 66, 69, 86, 89, 150, 162, 165, 167, 168, 169, 171, 173, 184, 185
investigation 5, 9, 65

J

Jesus 2, 14, 38, 41, 42, 43, 44, 47, 48, 50, 51, 52, 54, 84, 85, 93, 94, 95, 97, 98, 104, 110, 114, 117, 119, 121, 123, 124, 148, 153, 156, 157, 158, 159, 165
John Wesley 55, 56

K

kidnapping 27, 52, 115
Koinonia 82

L

Lausanne Movement 35, 182
limitedness 81
Linkages 135
liturgical 36, 54, 55, 83, 93
liturgy 41, 47, 83, 95
lockdown 3, 4, 9, 11, 17, 23, 24, 25, 26, 27, 29, 30, 32, 33, 74, 76, 100, 101, 102, 103, 104, 107, 109, 110, 112, 113, 116, 119, 120, 121, 122, 126, 127, 139, 140, 143, 146, 147, 149, 153, 158, 159, 161, 164, 181
Lordship 84

M

magnitude 6
Margaret Gowans 128
marketplace 70, 162
media 5, 62, 67, 68, 69, 70, 71, 72, 73, 87, 103, 105, 107, 108, 109, 110, 115, 122, 125, 133, 140, 141, 142, 143, 144, 148, 149, 153, 158
medicine 6, 72
Mediterranean 12, 67, 169
metropolis 3
milieu 38, 39, 43, 70
Minister's Handbook 79, 83, 84, 93, 94, 95, 176
Ministry 2, 78
miracles 58, 73, 79, 156
misleading 88, 124, 133, 153
missiological 8, 40
mission xii, 43, 59, 77, 81, 85, 86, 88, 89, 97, 98, 99, 104, 123, 126, 127, 129, 130, 131, 132, 148, 152
missionary 42, 54, 87, 88, 91, 114, 121, 128, 131
Missionary ix, x, 17, 36, 38, 40, 64, 86, 131, 169, 175

models 124, 161
monitoring 5, 146
monumental 12
muzzled 6
mystical 51

N

NCDC x, 3
Nigeria ix, x, 1, 2, 4, 5, 7, 9, 16, 24, 25, 26, 27, 28, 29, 30, 31, 32, 33, 36, 62, 63, 64, 65, 66, 67, 69, 70, 73, 75, 76, 86, 89, 91, 92, 93, 103, 105, 106, 107, 108, 112, 114, 115, 116, 119, 124, 127, 128, 131, 132, 134, 138, 143, 144, 146, 147, 152, 153, 154, 155, 156, 157, 158, 165, 166, 170, 171, 173, 175, 176, 177, 179, 180, 182, 184

O

obstructive 6
Okada 25, 30
opulent 154
orthodoxy 80
outburst 5
Outreach 2

P

palliatives 25, 107, 108, 143, 144
pandemic 3, 4, 7, 8, 9, 10, 11, 12, 15, 16, 17, 24, 25, 26, 27, 28, 29, 30, 31, 32, 33, 75, 76, 103, 109, 111, 112, 113, 122, 127, 143, 184
paradigms 71, 72
patient 5, 6
Pentecostal 36, 53, 54, 55, 56, 57, 58, 59, 60, 61, 62, 63, 65, 66, 67, 68, 69, 71, 72, 73, 77, 79, 80, 96, 110, 133, 140, 141, 142, 149, 154, 166, 167, 168, 169, 173, 175
Pentecostalism 16, 53, 54, 55, 57, 58, 59, 60, 61, 62, 63, 65, 67, 68, 69, 70, 71, 72, 73, 77, 80, 88, 133, 134, 141, 166, 167, 169, 170, 171, 172, 174, 175, 179
persecutions 14, 120
PHEIC x, 10
phenomenon 27, 35, 45, 57, 70, 139, 142, 161
philosophy 150, 151
physician 6, 13
pietistic 46
pilgrim 38, 39, 40
pilgrimage xi, 39, 48, 51, 149
plague 12, 13, 14, 15, 154, 180, 183, 185
pneumatic 57
political impunity 115
populace 4, 150
portraiture 150
precipitated 4, 114, 121
Presbyterian 128
press 3, 5

principle 38, 39, 82, 98, 121
Professor xii, 4, 5, 6, 7, 70, 75
proliferated 65
Prosperity 71, 123, 153, 155, 156, 157, 158, 165, 183
Prosperity Theology 71
Protestant 36
Protestantism 16, 41
pseudo 73
Psyche 73
pulmonary 6

Q

quietistic 51

R

Radio ELWA 87, 93, 122, 132, 139
reality 3, 38, 40, 92, 105, 123, 149, 158
recession 26
reckless 2
redemption 81, 97, 159
reformation 124, 157
Reformation 55
religiosity 116
religious 7, 15, 23, 27, 43, 50, 52, 60, 61, 62, 63, 67, 69, 70, 71, 72, 76, 101, 107, 112, 113, 114, 115, 116, 124, 131, 138
research 6, 8, 9, 65, 125, 141
respiratory 6, 10, 11
reverence 77, 83, 90
revolutionary 9

Roman 12, 13, 36, 53, 61, 70
Rowland Bingham 128, 130, 132

S

sacrament 38, 47
sacrificial 14, 15, 17, 97, 159
salvation 2, 43, 45, 46, 48, 51, 54, 57, 85, 87, 91, 94, 97, 117, 122, 125
Salvation Army 128
schism 36, 37
Scholars 13, 60, 62, 68, 132
scholarship 8, 57
scourge 7, 8
Scripture x, 44, 45, 46, 89, 96
sectionalism 36, 37, 40
Seleucia 13
Service leadership 78
settlement 1, 2
SIM x, 87, 95, 129, 130, 131, 138, 166, 173
sin 2, 72, 124, 133, 150, 153, 155, 156, 158, 164
smallpox 13
Social Capital 60, 132, 134, 135, 138, 169
social-distancing 4, 101, 181
Social Distancing 101
sociological 8
sowing 79
Success 124
Sudan x, 129, 130, 132, 135, 168, 169

suspension 5, 32
symbols 72

T

tapestry 9, 37, 43, 73
Tapestry 60
taxonomy 56
Teaching x, 4, 76, 180
technology 8, 74, 148
televangelism 88
television 2, 73, 107, 108, 153, 180
Territory x, 4
theological 8, 40, 42, 54, 55, 57, 67, 88, 104, 131, 143, 157, 162
Thomas Kent 128, 130
Today's Challenge 87, 91
tongues 17, 54, 55, 57, 59, 79, 151
Topeka, Kansas 55
transformation 3, 38, 41, 51, 99
transnational 67
tropicalizing 87
tuberculosis 6

U

Ubuntu 150, 151, 171
UITH x, 4, 5, 7
uncivil 2
Unemployment 26
UNESCO 31
unethical 5
Uniformity 79
University x, xii, 4, 14, 41, 57, 61, 65, 68, 70, 76, 83, 88, 125, 132, 167, 168, 170, 171, 172, 174, 175
unprecedented 7, 8, 53, 60, 67, 75, 102
unquenchable 124
Ushers 78

V

Vineyard 2
violent 79
vision 45, 51, 88, 127, 128, 130
vulnerable 25, 34, 143, 144, 145, 146

W

Walter Gowans 128, 130, 132
war-oriented 79
wartime 87
WASSC x, 1
watershed 130
way-ward 2
Wesleyan 129
worldliness 2
Worldliness 124
worldviews 14, 15, 70, 72
worship 3, 9, 43, 55, 67, 74, 76, 77, 78, 79, 80, 81, 82, 83, 84, 85, 90, 91, 92, 93, 95, 96, 97, 98, 99, 102, 103, 104, 105, 108, 109, 110, 113, 116, 118, 120, 124, 127, 140, 144, 147, 148, 149, 159, 162, 181
Wuhan 10, 11, 111

Lightning Source UK Ltd.
Milton Keynes UK
UKHW011010210820
368606UK00001B/232